The Two Farms

'The Hill', Trunch

The Two Farms

JOAN BAIN

ROBERT HALE · LONDON

First published in Great Britain 1989

Robert Hale Limited
Clerkenwell House
Clerkenwell Green
London EC1R 0HT

British Library Cataloguing in Publication Data

Bain, Joan, *1910–*
The Two Farms
1. Norfolk. North Norfolk. Agricultural industries. Farms. Social life 1910–1936
I. Title
924.6′12′083
ISBN 0–7090–3718–X

Photoset in North Wales by
Derek Doyle & Associates, Mold, Clwyd.
Printed in Great Britain by
St Edmundsbury Press Ltd, Bury St Edmunds, Suffolk.
Bound by WBC Bookbinders Limited.

Contents

Illustrations

All illustrations drawn by Roger Pearce

To my daughter, Jean

Loading hay

1. *Introducing the Theme*

Nowadays, when the years immediately after the First World War have become part of what children call 'olden times', there are some parents and teachers who like to drag the near past out of its historical context and use it to bolster up their social theories. But anyone who, like myself, was about ten years old in 1920 and can remember everyday events against the background of their communities finds that these versions of the life we lived may not at all agree with our own experience.

I was a farmer's child, the eldest of a family of four, who was born and brought up in a north Norfolk village. Nearly seventy years later, I thought I would like to write about the place and its people as I knew them in 1920, or earlier. I belonged to that place and people, for both my parents were born in Trunch and came of farming stock. Mother lived in the village all her life, and after father decided to settle down, he occupied the same farm from 1905 until he died in 1974, at the age of ninety-six. As many of father's relations lived to be over ninety and were blessed with excellent memories, I had a chance of hearing a great deal about the village as it had been in earlier days; so I have tried to use some of this material as a background to my own recollections and establish the whole as part of a continuing pattern of rural life.

Although every village in Norfolk may be said to have developed along its own lines, an agricultural way of life dictated the general direction of the development. Broadly speaking, Trunch was representative of most of the larger north Norfolk parishes of the post-1914–18 era, when war memories were close and the great twentieth-century changes in agriculture still part of the future. By giving a day-to-day view of the way we lived, I have tried to create a verbal picture of the two farmhouses and their occupants in the context of a village and its people. Nostalgia is bound to crop up on occasion, but the book is a sincere attempt to convey a tiny facet of social history through a distillation of personal, as well as family, recollections.

In 1920, the average Norfolk village was an individual little community which depended upon the land for its livelihood. Hand work, horse work and hard work were the order of the day. It was a way of life where every man had a job, although the job was often poorly paid. Social distinctions were complex, but everyone, however humble or half-witted, had a place in that society. As established families did not often move away and as means of getting about were limited, each parish remained very much a world of its own – a focus for corporate pride and, on occasion, for corporate silence. It is difficult for an outsider to grasp the intricate web of family relationships that helped to produce such communities, or to comprehend the mutual interdependence and basic understanding created by conditions of living and working together within the framework of a village. Our social differences and conventions were typical of the period, but the 'them and us' situation was considerably modified, because we knew so much about each other and shared the same rural background.

All of us were children of the land from the time we drew breath. As soon as we were able to walk, we enjoyed a common heritage in the beauty of the Norfolk countryside. On hot days we buried our small noses among the daisies in a patch of grass and breathed in the intoxicating aroma of growth. We experienced the feel of the furrows under our feet and the prick of the stubble that bloodied our ankles. We felt at home with the land. There was no place in rural life for those who did not.

The land at Trunch was not part of a great country estate, and those farmers who were tenants remained independent as long as they paid their rent and kept on good terms with absentee landlords, who wanted only a return on their investments. The parish, which had a population of nearly 400, contained a total of 1,357 acres divided into nine main farms and a number of smaller holdings of a few acres apiece. To a certain extent, our lives were still under the influence of Victorian values: children were told in a rather pious way that the better off should set an example to others and that, the more you had the more you should be prepared to do for the community. Farmers were no exception.

The general idea was that, after King and Country, a farmer's immediate loyalties should be to his family, then to his labourers, their families and the village as a whole. It was understood that those who farmed the land had the greatest duty (not necessarily a monetary one) towards the parish, and the majority of them accepted this unwritten responsibility. To a farmer's child, the village people were a kind of extension of the family circle at a different level, and, as with my numerous relatives, there were some I knew better than others and some I did not know at all. In various ways, we all served the land and lived under the discipline of our involvement. It was an economic necessity for us to do so.

It was an economic necessity for a farmer to look after himself and his family. He was his own master, received no State support and was totally independent of everything except the weather, yet he had to live with the knowledge that, unless he had money put by, crop failures, low prices or illness could make bankruptcy the price of independence. The village poor had a very hard time of it – in a way that only those who are now old can understand. A constant effort was made to help the sick and families with large numbers of children, but it was important that this should be done with tact. Mother knew the village people, and anything she sent out was regarded as a gift from a friend; but, at the other extreme, there was a well-meaning meddler whose 'little presents' were received with silent resentment – accepted only because, however much the recipients might detest charity and condescension, they knew they were too poor to be choosy.

Norfolk people were by nature individual and independent. In general, they were slow to anger but never forgot a bad turn or times when they had been given a helping hand. Eccentricity was tolerated – even admired – and, among stories relating to the County families, we heard about a Walpole who drove red deer four-in-hand and a Windham who became a coachman. The Norfolk dialect (of which I have tried to give an indication), with many of the old words and expressions, was in everyday use. Religion was important, and the virtues of hard work, honesty and cleanliness were amongst those advocated in the Bible, as well as being an essential adjunct to the way we lived. Many of the inhabitants were superstitious, though few of them would confess to a belief in ghosts. Instead, they agreed that, 'There might be something in it.'

In my own family, there were so many aunts and uncles, as well as great-aunts and great-uncles, that our relationships were almost tribal. In general, we grew up in a world which was controlled by the male members of the family, though a wife had her own place and authority, and a good husband saw to it that she retained her status if it was in any way encroached on by friends, family or employees. For one of us to be rude to mother was a cardinal sin, but to be rude to father was unthinkable.

Given the context of the period and the importance of physical strength, it seemed natural enough that ours should be a male-orientated society. There were exceptions: a small, shrewish woman, who used her sharp tongue to subordinate an enormous, easy-going husband, and a village amazon (also the dominant partner in marriage) who was described as being 'as strong as a man'. Of a well-known and successful but unmarried woman farmer, it was said that she should have been born a boy; and, in the agricultural world, she was treated as if she were a man.

The Pankhursts and the Suffragette movement were not in favour with countrymen. Any attempt at conversation on the subject was usually brought to a swift end by a masculine remark, like, 'Of course, they are all mad, anyway!' But when a favourite aunt and uncle were staying with us, I noticed that, although mother and aunt remained silent when one of the men made a slightly contemptuous reference to Emmeline

Pankhurst, an unspoken signal travelled between them, as if they thought they knew better. The talk changed course, but it was a new experience to feel that father and mother did not always agree with each other.

Regardless of social changes, the past conditioned the present in a way it does not today. In part, our lives appeared to be regulated by long-established rules, and many of the older people were suspicious of new labour-saving devices. They were convinced that doing it the hard way was the only means of achieving good work as well as job satisfaction, and were always ready to quote from a store of time-honoured sayings designed to fit any situation. Constant repetition of these rural proverbs implanted them in a child's mind for ever; it may also have encouraged closed minds, slow thinking and mental laziness, making it difficult to accept new ideas and innovations – 'Daylight Saving' was one of them.

The hardships and sorrows of war had been accepted as a patriotic necessity, but when 'Daylight Saving' was introduced, country folk could not find a good word to say about it. They believed it to be entirely for the benefit of city people. Farmers and their men resented the arbitrary disturbance of working hours. They said that Nature did not change to suit the new summer time: when the men arrived in the morning, there was too much dew about for them to make a start. At first, the greater part of the village tried to observe two times – 'God's time' (as they called it) for the farm and 'Government time' for other matters – but when anyone wanted to catch a train or make an appointment at North Walsham or Norwich, things became so complicated that in the end the parish found it easier to adjust to the new regime.

In 1920, memories of the late war were still very much a part of adult life. Everyone agreed that the world had become a different place and that things would never be the same again. There were those who appeared to see the pre-1914 days as if through a golden haze. Life (they said) had been astonishingly stable and contented – and everything so much better made, as well as costing half the price.

Farm labourers were not so sure. They said they supposed times were better than they had been in the past, for if a man asked his wife: 'What's for dinner?' and she replied 'Bread and Pullit', they both had a laugh. But what was only a wry joke in 1920 had meant bitter reality to some households during the lean years of the late nineteenth century.

2. *The Farmhouses and the Village*

The Great War disrupted but did not destroy the continuity of village life. When the celebratory anguish and rejoicing of the Armistice was over, the inhabitants of Trunch returned to the fields. They mourned their dead and did not parade their grief. Like their fathers before them, they said little but set to work and wove their sorrows into the pattern of an agricultural existence. The majority of them were essentially honest, decent, kindly people who knew how to make a little go a long way.

The size of the fields in which they ploughed and harvested varied between a 'piece' of anything up to ten or fifteen acres and the smallest half-acre or quarter-acre 'pightle'. Every field had its own name and its own characteristics. All of them were enclosed by banks and hedges whose height and thickness depended upon the activities of the farmer. The trees in the hedges and in the little plantations were so numerous that, viewed from a distance, one might have supposed us to be surrounded by woodland. The gnarled, ancient oaks on unsheltered roadsides carried few branches to the north-east; even at the height of summer their mutilated outlines bore silent witness to the force and sharpness of the sea wind. 'Come March, that there wind blow streat from Russia!' declared the old people.

If it was a closed landscape, it was also an intimate one. Before I was ten, I knew every corner of the farm and was familiar with most of the roads, lanes, plantations, ponds and pit-holes in the parish. When the Sunday morning sermon was dull or the prayers seemed endless, I used to recite field names to myself. Beginning at home with Stackyard Piece and The Rookery, I would let my mind travel the Southrepps road

South-west view of the church

to Marlhole and Ingham, return via Crossways Piece to Double Gates and Hilderbush on the Gimingham road, and end up with Ironsnek and Winding Furlongs on the way to Mundesley. One lovely summer morning, my grandfather was not in his usual pew: 'I have been to see Parson Greenfields,' he informed me, later on, and I thought I could detect a twinkle in his eye.

My father and grandfather occupied the farms known as White House and Ivy House, which had been standing side by side along the Mundesley road for several hundred years. A high brick wall separated the gardens of the two houses, and an older but equally high stone wall between our garden and the road bore the date 1696. A more elaborate '1775' was incorporated in the patterned brickwork at the back of grandfather's stables. It is probable that some kind of dwellings had existed on the site for centuries before those dates.

Over the years, the houses had been enlarged and improved, the farmyards shifted to one side and lawns and shrubberies planted in front. In the earlier part of the nineteenth century, White House was bought by mother's grandfather, an excellent businessman in his youth but reputedly eccentric in old age. Although his death occurred in 1881, there were many tales still told of him in the village. After he had gone to bed, they said, his sons would get out the bottles and foregather round the table in the time-honoured manner. The sideboard that held their liquor became a familiar object to us when it stood in an uncle's dining-room, but it was not until long afterwards that I discovered that the interesting little cupboard set in one end of it had been designed to hold a chamber pot, and so saved my ancestors many cold trips outside on winter nights.

When bad times came to the farming community in the nineties, those who spent too much money and were not brought up to hard work went to the wall, and White House passed into other hands until father rented it soon after his return from the Boer War.

Although mother's family was known to have lived in Trunch since the fifteenth century and a direct male line has been recorded from the early seventeenth century, their gradual rise in the world appeared to reach its apogee in the career of her grandfather. He ended up by owning and improving the greater part of the parish and, incidentally, did a very useful job for the future by redistributing some of the scattered fields, leaving each farm as a more compact unit.

Father's forebears had come up in the world at a later date. His first Norfolk ancestor was believed to have arrived as a migrant shoemaker from Hampshire during the latter part of the eighteenth century. The shoemaker settled near Field Dalling, and here his descendants established a gradual footing on the land, until, in 1896, my paternal grandfather became owner of part of the Trunch property that had once belonged to mother's relations.

Where records are available, it is interesting to study the ebb and flow of village social history. Once out of the strait-jacket of the feudal system, there must always have been this movement of individuals and families in rural England. Over the centuries, those with the necessary luck or ability rose from the lower echelons of society like slow bubbles in a pot of country broth, while others who had been better off sank to rejoin the essential elements below the surface.

Outside our immediate family and farm, the village surrounded our young lives. Good or bad, we were all members of a community. When we stood at the yard gate, we could look beyond the pond and the parish pump to the Hill, once the site of a medieval market-place but now the open apex of a triangle enclosing the fine fifteenth-century church and a thatched public house. Front Street ran along the south side of the churchyard wall, and Back Street to the north of it. Nearly all the buildings were joint products of the local earth or the sea shore. The red bricks had been baked in a brickyard beside the parish clay, while innumerable loads of stones were carted, from either the land or nearby beaches, to provide material for some of the cottages and all the cobbled walls. At varying heights, these walls surrounded the gardens and buildings of little house and big house alike, making an agreeably cohesive pattern of the parish centre.

Trunch was a compact village as Norfolk villages go. Apart from a few isolated dwellings, the houses of the remainder of the population were divided between Chapel Road, where there was a small Methodist and an even smaller Wesleyan chapel, and Brewery Road, where a tall, red-brick chimney and the scent of hops guided one to what might have been called our village industrial site. Using the same matter-of-fact nomenclature, other outgoing roads were known by the names of the parishes to which they led. Mundesley, Knapton, North Walsham, Bradfield, Southrepps and Gimingham were the immediate boundaries of our parochial horizon. If some of the smaller lanes and lokes had their origins in the long past, their names had been much changed by time and the eccentricities of the Norfolk dialect.

In 1920, the inhabitants of a small village did not have far to go to do their shopping. Trunch was served by three general stores – one of which housed His Majesty's Post Office, and their piled-up shelves contained everything from bacon and cheese to lamp wicks, paraffin, clothes and knitting-wool. We had two butchers' shops – one of them sold nothing but pork, and summer visitors spoke ecstatically of his sausages. Both men did their own slaughtering in buildings behind the shops. Milk was supplied by two small farmers who made daily deliveries in separate parts of the parish; if a customer ran short, it was easy enough to take an empty jug or can round to the farmer's back door. These facilities were supplemented by visits from a fisherman who smoked kippers and bloaters as well as selling fresh, locally caught fish (the sea is only two miles away), and by sundry individuals driving little carts who brought home-grown vegetables and an assortment of groceries to the doorstep. Two of our shop-keepers went on this kind of round and visited outlying parishes. Because of the general use of oil lamps, paraffin was one of the staple commodities in every household, and over the years one of these men must have sold hundreds of gallons of the precious liquid and opened and closed the tap of the tank on his cart thousands of times. He was a pillar of the Methodist church and much respected, but behind his back he was known as 'Paraffin Pike'.

The village had no baker, but the shops had a choice of three local bakeries from which to receive a daily supply of bread for re-sale. The bread sold in the village was nearly all in large white loaves, plus a quantity of lovely cottage loaves with crusty, bun-shaped tops. Mother always made her own bread, so, in the perverse way of children everywhere, a baker's loaf was a real treat in our house.

The tradesmen looked after their business to the best of their inclinations or abilities. So did the blacksmith who shod the farm horses, and the carpenter and wheelwright, the bricklayer and the well-sinker. The whole countryside was full of the kinds of skills and knowledge that have passed into history.

When a man was no longer able to earn a living by the use of his particular skill or knowledge, the harsh realitites of country life forced him to abandon it and take up something else. If you looked around you, there were indications of skills that had already passed from the village. Many years ago, a man called Jarvis, a tailor, had painted his name and trade in huge black letters high on the wall of a house on the Hill. The words 'JARVIS – TAILOR' remained there for all to see, but we knew no one who remembered Jarvis. A memory of the past was often perpetuated in a field name. The Trunch brickyards had been closed at some time during the war and were never reopened. Father bought Brickyard Piece, which contained the remains of the smaller of the two businesses. The brickmaker had occupied a corner of the field where a large, overgrown area surrounded the pit from which he had dug his clay. The whole place looked as if one day the man had suddenly downed tools and departed, leaving behind him the clay pit and his little sheds and kiln, as well as a pile of good red bricks.

Malthouse Pightle was a two-acre field behind the remains of a building in use as a malthouse in the early days of Trunch Brewery. In 1837, mother's grandfather decided to build a brewery in the grounds of an agreeable house of which he was the owner. Later on, one of his sons lived in the house and ran the business. Beer was cheap, and enormous quantities of it were drunk in the country, especially during the strenuous days of haysel (the hay-making season) and harvest. It was said that men could not work without beer. As the picturesque 'Crown' on the Hill was not under my great-grandfather's control, he built the 'New Inn' at the corner of Chapel Road. It was all a bit like one of our nursery jingles: 'He farmed the land that grew the best barley, the best of his barley was sent to his maltster, his brewery used the malt to brew the beer, the beer was sold at his public house and bought by the men who grew the barley.' If he tried to grow his own hops, there is no record of it.

By 1920, the New Inn as well as the Crown was owned by other breweries and, as there was no public house at either Gimingham or Knapton and plenty of beer-drinkers at Trunch, the two houses were not short of customers. In my youth, the tenant of the New Inn was Mr Royall, a short, thick-set man with a drooping moustache. He was also the owner of a black cab drawn by a sturdy type of horse in which he drove passengers when they wished to attend a local funeral or catch a train at North Walsham. To drive behind Royall when he was wearing his black frock-coat and top hat was quite a prestigious experience. When not in use, the old horse could be seen surveying the open inn yard, its head thrust out over the top of the stable door.

In 1914 a parish hall had been erected by public subscription on glebeland opposite the rectory, but the building of a cobble-walled village school in 1853 was assisted by a more ancient form of giving. My grandfather told us that the parish farmers carted stones from Mundesley beach in order to provide their contribution to village education. As a boy, he had helped in the work. Years later, his sons learned to read and write and do their sums within its walls and were probably not too keen when the time came for them to go to North Walsham Grammar School. They walked four miles there and four miles back in every sort of weather. At sixteen, they were considered to have enough book-learning and were expected to return to the farm or find their opportunities elsewhere. The four sons travelled far and at times lived hard, but wherever they settled, they farmed the land.

A game of croquet

3. *The Farmhouses and Their Gardens*

The two farmhouses and their occupants had been always as much accessories of the land as the ploughs in the farmyards or the horses in the stables. 'There is never a separate price put on a farmhouse,' said my father. 'If a farm is sold, the house just goes along with the land.'

When one of the great steam-engines drawing threshing-tackle passed by along the Mundesley road, the old houses would shudder and rattle their windows as if in protest against the vibrations. A stranger might have supposed their condition to be dangerous. Ivy House gave the impression of being the better kept of the two – possibly because it was my grandfather's own property. Although, basically, White House must have been sound enough, the subject of its external repairs was inclined to linger in the ill-defined area that exists between a tenant's requirements and the length of his landlord's purse. Because the roof leaked in a number of places, old chamber pots, basins and pails were never thrown away as long as they would hold water. Up to the attics they went, to be arranged in strategic positions all ready to catch the drips from the roof and prevent water passing through the attic floor to the bedrooms below. If, as occasionally happened, some water managed to escape its container and penetrate the floor, mother said that it was sure to emerge upon a freshly whitewashed ceiling. This may have caused her considerable distress, but it was a way of life to her children. It was not until we were some years older that we realized that a leaking roof was not necessarily a commonplace in the homes of our contemporaries.

It was said of a previous owner that whenever he tided over a bad year by taking in paying guests, his children had to move into the attics. We had no such familiarity with what was to us a mysterious and unfrequented part of the house; so, if we found the door of the back staircase open to the kitchen, it was like a challenge to adventure. The bare, scrubbed wooden stairs corkscrewed beyond a first-floor bedroom, then continued upwards, their open treads exactly like the steep ascent from the barn to the granary. On incurably wet days, the weekly wash was pegged to long lines strung all about the attic storey. A wet Monday was not a popular occasion, for it was awkward to carry so many sheets and pillowcases up the narrow stairs; but at least the linen was out of the kitchen and, with any necessary opening and shutting of the dormer windows, could be left to dry at leisure.

An attic floor was a natural repository for the overflow of a country household. Very little was ever thrown away, because it was believed that anything might come in handy sometime. Boxes of old clothes and piles of ancient fashion magazines illustrating ladies with hour-glass waists and swan-like, Edwardian bosoms represented my parents' surplus at that period, but my grandparents' attic store was more extensive. One could stumble over the remains of discarded four-poster beds and tables and chairs swathed in outworn sheets. There were innumerable brimming trunks and – most fascinating of all – long, pigeon-holed shelves stacked with neatly tied remnants of silk and cotton material. the aftermath of years of home dressmaking. The inroads of moth and woodworm were kept in check but could not be eradicated.

The size and shape of the houses suggested a pattern of continued alteration and improvement of the original dwellings. The south bedrooms at White House had doors leading from one room to another, as well as doors giving access to a narrow passage running east to west. Two little rooms on the north side of this passage were lean-to above the pantry and dairy; their sloping ceilings were so low that the windowsills were on the floor, and one could only crouch beside them. At ground level, the way from the front door passed through the chimney-breast between dining-room and drawing-room to meet a passage from the back door at the foot of a wide stairway. Omitting the cellar and attic storey in a count of living and storerooms, you achieved a total of five first-floor rooms with a storeroom and dairy and seven bedrooms, plus a dressing-room equipped with two tin baths and a flush lavatory off the landing half-way up the stairs. But, to anyone familiar with the average Norfolk farmhouse and its conglomeration of kitchen premises and small rooms tacked on here and there, the result was far from imposing, but homely, and necessitated a great deal of domestic labour as well as the continuous use of one's legs.

Ivy House appeared to have developed on much the same lines, although the treatment of its eastern end was somewhat different, and the ceilings of the north bedrooms were of normal height. Upstairs, my grandmother had a real bathroom with a long bath, a washbasin and a flush lavatory. Even when there was no means of heating it, it was a luxury to have cold water piped upstairs: the expectant bather had only to carry up a pailful of hot water from the kitchen and, when ablutions were completed, he or she could rejoice in the labour-saving device of pulling out the plug and watching the used bathwater disappear.

A ground-floor lavatory might have been regarded as a link between an old-fashioned outside privy and its indoor successor: a door near the foot of the staircase opened into a high-walled enclosure which was open to the sky, while another door in the wall across this paved area gave access to a dry closet. Children found it a very spooky place at dusk.

Although most of the larger farmhouses possessed a flush lavatory, at a period when water might have to be pumped up by hand it was convenient to retain the older, outside privies for limited use. The approach to White House's 'Jericho', as Parson Woodforde called those edifices, ran beside a high stone wall, along a path bordered by violets and purple flag iris. At a polite distance from the house, it was not so far that a swift sortie through the rain became too unpleasant. A window above the door lighted a range of two large wooden seats with a smaller one between them. It was possible to imagine that this had once been quite a sociable place. In my day, it was occupied in decent seclusion, and the smaller aperture contained only sawdust and some toilet paper. For reasons of economy, an outdated Jarold's railway time-table (then a thick little book) was laid out for additional use. On the other side of the wall was a separate apartment for the maids or women working in the house. Both places were kept scrupulously clean and the brick floors scrubbed once a week.

When necessary, the containers were emptied through low doors at the rear which opened into a fenced cesspit near the pig yard. A drain from the flush lavatory in the house ran into the same area, and the pit was cleaned out about once a year by the yard man. A cheerful individual, with a healthy liking for a drink, he downed a good shot of rum before and a larger one on completion of his task. Nothing ever appeared to go wrong with the system, and it continued to function until mains water was laid on to the house in the late 1940s.

Before the advent of mains water, when a countryman spoke of water being 'laid on', it was taken for granted that the supply came from a well belonging to his house. We often gathered round the outside pump in the morning to watch Bob, the yard man, as he raised and lowered the heavy iron handle, and, with him, counted the strokes that were necessary to fill the tank above the lavatory roof. When water dripped from the overflow, the job was done for the day, and woe betide the child who pulled the chain too lavishly and emptied the tank before its time. After he had pumped up, Bob filled a number of white enamel pails which were reserved for drinking and cooking-water and carried them indoors to the dairy.

In common with the rest of the parish, we were dependent upon direct rainfall for the major part of our water supply. Every drop that fell on the south side of the house roof was channelled into either an underground cistern or one of two circular corrugated-iron tanks near the back door. A hand pump attached to the wall at one end of the scullery sink brought up water from the cistern, which, if required, could be supplemented from one or other of the tanks. Sometimes, in hot weather, a little red worm bred in the cistern and caused considerable excitement when it was discovered in the bathwater. All the gutters and downpipes at the back of the house ended in small tanks or barrels. There was little water wasted and – in a dry period – little margin for waste.

The kitchen arrangements of a farmhouse in 1920 would appear positively archaic today. Although the open hearth over which pots and kettles could be suspended had long been superseded by the closed range, my grandmother's back kitchen still contained an open fireplace, with the old hooks and chains hanging inside the chimney. Food for the chickens was sometimes cooked upon it. The expression 'black as the hakes', which was in everyday use, took on a new meaning when one peered through the wood smoke to look at the soot-encrusted iron fitments above.

At White House, mother's scullery (or 'back kitchen', as it was called) contained a large, shallow sink and a copper for boiling 'the whites'; all the smaller paraffin lamps and some candlesticks were kept at one end of a wooden table standing against a wall, and above them were rows of cast-iron or enamel saucepans and frying-pans on high shelves. The front kitchen looked more comfortable. If the big wooden dresser and a corner cupboard for grocery were strictly functional, so was a pretty old clock hanging on a wall. The six shiny dishcovers above the dresser were in regular use, but the traditional hams and bacon and bunches of dried herbs no longer dangled from the hooks in the ceiling beam. After dinner, our little maid covered the table top with a dark-red cloth and placed a rag rug on the brick floor before the range; when she opened the fire and drew up her armchair for an afternoon sit-down, it made quite a cosy picture.

It is often the little things in life that rouse a child's curiosity, and the nicely graduated row of bells which hung along the kitchen passage was one such object. We could ring the appropriate bell from the front door and the dining-room, or by pulling a red-tasselled cord in the drawing-room or in the spare bedroom. But there were so many bells! Was it likely that every room in the house had once had its own bell or that there had ever been enough occupants of the kitchen to answer them? Later on in life, one suspected that a good row of bells in a passage might have been a nineteenth-century farmhouse status symbol.

The dairy was dim and cold, with long stone or wooden shelves and a meat safe covered in wire gauze at the window end. The pantry was large enough to hold all the household silver and china as well as three floor-to-ceiling food cupboards. On baking days, the shelves of these cupboards were filled with a spendid assortment of fruit pies, cakes and pastries in sufficient quantity to keep the family going for another week.

Our dining-room was also the family sitting-room, except on Sundays or special occasions. This was the usual country custom. Farmhouse dining-rooms were large, with a table in proportion, and parents could settle into armchairs on either side of the fireplace while their children used the big table for games or writing or school homework. We had a leather-covered sofa on which it was very comfortable to lie if one felt sick or had the beginnings of a headache; bedrooms were usually unheated, and one felt isolated in them during the day.

It is indicative of the sturdy qualities of Victorian and Edwardian furniture that, at the ages of about five to eight, we were able to play a game known as 'Walking round the dining-room on the furniture'. To touch the floor was to admit failure, so we swung on doors or curtains and crawled over the chairs and sideboard without causing any apparent damage, while the stags on the surrounding Landseer prints appeared to regard our antics with sardonic indifference. The game was restricted to rainy days when all other amusements failed and the rest of the household was too busy or exhausted to bother.

The pictures in the drawing-room were of a different nature – Queen Victoria's Drawing-Room, Napoleon Buonaparte, the Battle of Sebastopol and a Madonna and Child. The chairs were slightly more comfortable, and the furniture was not so dark and heavy. On Sundays, if we sat around with mother after dinner, she would produce quite exciting books of Bible stories or a few special toys out of the

Sunday cupboard. Sometimes she would play the piano. All in all, the day was pleasantly different, and I think that the drawing-room exerted a civilizing influence.

Children were not allowed in the room that father used as an office. The only time it could be swept or dusted was on a Saturday morning when he was at Norwich. Even then, the task was performed with the utmost caution, for, though father did not appear to notice dust, he would raise the roof if he found that his papers or books had been moved an inch or two from their accustomed places. As just about every farmer in the area visited Norwich on Saturdays in order to buy or sell bullocks at the cattle market or to sell their corn at the Corn Hall, it is probable that many other Norfolk office rooms underwent a surreptitious cleaning on that day.

Farmhouse gardens were rambling and, by modern standards, extensive. One or two acres was the usual size. There was always a rather unkempt shrubbery, with lilacs and laburnums, laurels and viburnum tinus – all stretching skyward, while, below, the bare boughs arched like a roof above the dark earth. A shrubbery was a good place for children's play-houses and hidey-holes – if you were not afraid of the gloom. In addition, the gardens included beds for flowers, lawns used for bowls, croquet or tennis, a separate enclosure (often walled) for vegetables and an orchard. Beautiful plums, pears, peaches and figs could be grown against some of those old walls.

The area devoted to a kitchen garden was always geared to the needs of a large family. If the household was a small one, the surplus produce was given away. On the other hand, when a previous owner of White House took in paying guests, he planted up part of an adjacent pasture in order to cope with the increased demand on his fruit and vegetables. Twenty years after his departure and the subsequent demise of his new garden, clumps of rhubarb were still to be seen among the grass.

These gardens were far from immaculate, as few farmers employed a regular gardener. They found it cheaper and easier to bring in a couple of men when work was slack in the fields. Potatoes and other vegetables might be planted at about the right time, but otherwise it tended to be the farmer's main interest that claimed the maximum attention. For some men, the chief concern might be a well-filled kitchen garden; for my father, it was his bowling-green, and everything else came a very bad second. Mother looked after the conservatory that opened out of the drawing-room, so her outside involvements did not go beyond two pink oleanders, a collection of pot plants and her chrysanthemums.

During the winter, tidy-minded orchard owners enjoyed the sight of hygienically whitewashed tree trunks, which were so treated to clean them of lichens and discourage insects hidden in the bark; one or two progressives applied grease bands designed to trap insects moving up or down but, beyond an occasional thinning when growth became too dense, father's trees received no such attention. While the apple crop was of considerable domestic importance, one of its rare failures was accepted with country philosophy: people said that there looked like being a lot of plums, the apples could do with a rest, and next year we would have plenty of them. In practice, because there was enough ground in which to plant about double the family requirements, crop failures were compensated for and an occasional absence of fruit kept certain pests in check.

The old orchards were planted in rich variety: plums and damsons, pears, walnuts, perhaps a medlar or a quince, but it was the apple that had pride of place. A little red July apple called Mr Gladstone opened the season; it turned yellow and red when it fell off the tree and, even if picked, lasted only a fortnight. Another early eating-apple was known as Maiden's Legs, though its cheerful pinkish stripes made it unlike any legs we had ever seen. Lord Suffield was a green cooker. There were some early Codlins which, together with the later Blenheim Orange, were suitable for either eating or cooking, while a big fallen tree called the Old Transparent remained propped in a horizontal position – it bore almost white fruit of a pleasant acidity. We also possessed a Norfolk Beefin and a huge, nameless tree bearing rusty-looking green cookers, so sour that they were used only when all else failed.

The Norfolk Beefin or Biffin was an old apple, said to have been introduced into this country from Normandy, where it may have been called Beaufin. Old people told us that there were three varieties, red, green and striped. It was a good cooker as well as a dessert apple and, if picked at the right time, would keep until early summer in the following year. The Biffin was renowned for its qualities as a baking apple and during the nineteenth century achieved epicurean fame as a dessert delicacy; the apples were placed between sheets of iron and dried very slowly in the baker's oven, and his appreciative customers ate them after dinner with an accompaniment of sugar and cream.

If one came across a burr knot tree in an old orchard or cottage garden, the owner liked to encourage a certain air of mystery about it. The trees I saw were either apples or plums and could be distinguished by rough, rusty swellings here and there upon the branches. The tree could be propagated and the burr knot characteristic perpetuated by cutting off and planting one of the knots. I remember a nameless dessert plum in the garden of White House: it was a burr knot tree, and the fruit was large, dark blue and meltingly sweet – quite unlike any other plum we knew. Because of the ease of propagation, it is possible that some burr-knot varieties may have been very old indeed.

Grandfather's orchard included a large cooking-apple tree whose branches were hung with heavy pieces of old iron. Years ago, the irons had been placed there to bring down the branches and get the tree into bearing. He had several russets, a juicy little Kerry Pippin, a Doctor Harvey and a most beautiful dark-red apple called Armorelle – rather acid when raw, but it cooked to a rosy foam. There were apples for all occasions from July to the following June; they were made into pies, puddings and dumplings, as well as baked or stewed. At the rectory, in the farms, shops and cottages, apples were a staple item in the diet of the entire population.

A 'good dry' on wash-day

4. *The Domestic Routine of the Farmhouse*

Many of the larger farmhouses kept two maids living in, but I do not remember mother having more than one.

Mother's young maid, Maud, was part of our lives, and we would have found it difficult to visualize the house without her. At the time, Maud must have been about fifteen. She slept in a back bedroom and had two half-days off a week. Because her home was in the village, she was often allowed out after tea, though the time set for her return had to be strictly adhered to. At first, it was eight or nine o'clock, but as she became older her hour was gradually extended to ten. A fourteen-year-old, fresh from day school and the teeming life of a crowded cottage, must have found going out to service an adventurous but, at the same time, rather a lonely change of life.

Honesty and cleanliness were prime considerations in choosing a young maid, and mother liked to engage a girl from one of the village families where those qualities were known to flourish. A girl who worked in her own parish had less reason for initial home-sickness and, because they were known to each other, it was easy for her mother and her mistress to discuss her welfare and keep her from 'going wrong'. 'Going wrong' in early girlhood often resulted in a baby, so it was a state to be avoided; though, if the event occurred, it was usually accepted with country commonsense and the child brought up as one of the family. Once a girl acquired a regular young man and started walking out with him, marriage became an obvious remedy for the demands of nature. Older women might put their heads closer together when they were gossiping across the low flint walls surrounding the cottages, and the talk might be of what they called 'force-work' and 'shotgun weddings', but, because there was always so much to gossip about, each individual item soon faded into local history.

Although my mother was regarded in the village as a lady to be looked up to, and though her help and advice were sought by many of the women, she was a farmer's wife and did not lead a sheltered, drawing-room type of existence with a bevy of servants at her beck and call. Looking back and remembering the hard, physical effort involved in running a farmhouse at that time, I think she must have been unendingly busy and that she organized the work with a minimum of outside help. Maud's mother arrived each Monday to do the family washing, and Bob, the yard man, brought in supplies of wood, coal and drinking-water. When mother had a baby due, the monthly nurse arrived, a relative came in to housekeep, and afterwards, while the child was very small, the wife of one of the farm men provided some extra help with cooking.

The women in the cottages were up by 5 a.m., in order that their men could get to work at six or six-thirty. We were not quite so early astir, though father liked to be in the yard to see the team man before the others arrived. Maud's alarm clock could be heard about six, for she had a good deal to accomplish before breakfast.

A maid's uniform was provided by her mistress and varied little (except in quality) from house to house. In the morning, Maud wore a blue print dress with a large white apron, and a white cap covered her hair. If there was really dirty work to be done, or while she was scrubbing floors, she used a dark, rougher type of apron; but after dinner she looked very smart indeed, when she had changed into her black dress, enlivened by a frivolous, lacy little white apron and cap to match.

There was nothing frivolous about Maud's morning uniform. It was a necessary protection as she 'did' first the kitchen range and then the dining-room grate, for coal fires in general and ranges in particular had an unfortunate habit of generating dust whenever they were poked. Paper and sticks had been left ready overnight, but before she could lay the fires, she had to black-lead and polish both grates. After the top of the range had been polished, it shone like black satin. Once the niceties of arranging crumpled newspapers, sticks and pieces of coal had been grasped, a welcome glow was the usual reward; but striking a match to light a fire was always a critical moment.

The range bore the date 1902. It stood in a wide recess which had contained an earlier system of open fire and wall ovens. Its flues were extensive and needed a weekly clean, using long, wire-handled brushes made for the purpose. If the soot in the flues was allowed to accumulate, the oven failed to heat in its usual reliable manner. In addition to whatever was cooking, the ample top held two or three iron kettles and an oval-shaped iron boiler for heating water. The oven was placed to the right of the central fire, while the left-hand side was occupied by an internal water tank which we filled by pouring cold water through a roundel in the upper surface; we drew off hot water by opening a brass tap at a lower level. Well above all this was an iron rack where plates could be heated or the bread put to rise.

When the range fire had been made up, the round plate above it was left open so that a kettle could boil there as quickly as possible. According to the time spent in cleaning the stove, the first pot of tea of the day could be produced in from half to three-quarters of an hour. Mother dressed the children and then cooked breakfast, while Maud swept and dusted the dining-room.

Breakfast was always a substantial meal. Packet cereals were unknown to us, but in winter we sometimes had porridge. Father would never touch it; he said he had eaten all the porridge he needed in his youth. He filled up with eggs and bacon or sausages, bread and butter and marmalade. If anyone wanted toast, we used a long toasting-fork to make it over the dining-room fire. Liver-and-bacon was a favourite Sunday breakfast dish, perhaps because it could be prepared in advance.

Our only household labour-saving devices were a Ewebank carpet sweeper, a very early type of vacuum cleaner (used only for spring cleaning) and a knife machine. The table knives were of steel, but not the stainless variety: after washing-up was finished, they were inserted in the slots of the knife machine and, after a turn or two of the handle, the blades shone like new.

Washing-up after a meal can still be a chore, but nowadays few people use an enamel basin placed in a wide, shallow sink or operate a hand pump to supply them with cold water. They do not have to bring kettles and pails full of hot water from the front to the back kitchen. This carrying of water about the house was a never-ending task, and a large collection of white enamel pails and jugs, as well as the brown cans designed to take hot water to the bedrooms, was needed for its constant circulation.

The array of paraffin lamps ranged from large brass table lamps to tiny nightlights, each with its white china shade, which children found so reassuring if they woke up at night. It was essential to keep the wicks trimmed and glass chimneys clean, and not to overfill the containers with paraffin. Mother usually cleaned the lamps while Maud 'did' the bedrooms. This daily task involved emptying wash-basins and slop-pails, then filling up water-bottles and jugs (hard water for teeth, soft for washing), scalding chamber pots and wiping down the marble-topped washstands. A separate cloth was used for each purpose: all to be washed later on and hung outside to dry ready for the next day.

A weekly routine was superimposed upon these everyday jobs. Rooms were turned out, stairs and landings swept and dusted. The stone or brick passage floors were scrubbed; so were the kitchen, the pantry and the dairy. The expression 'turning out a room' was not a misnomer at a time when chairs and smaller articles of furniture were stacked outside in a passage, the immovable, heavy pieces swathed in dustsheets and the carpet swept on hands and knees, using a stiff brush and a dustpan. It was inevitable that about a third of the dust rose into the air, thus proving the necessity for such arduous preparations.

If a brick floor was very dusty, it was sprinkled with water before sweeping began. When the bricks were worn and uneven, they were swept again after scrubbing to remove any fluff left by the 'dwile' or floorcloth. In our case, the dwile was made at home from a double thickness of flannel united by long stitches of wool. The edge of the cloth was left unsewn, because an even surface made for easier wringing out.

In the absence of a professional window-cleaner with a ladder, the only satisfactory way to clean the exterior of a bedroom window was by the practice known as 'sitting out'. A woman pushed up the lower part of one of the heavy sash-windows and twisted herself round until she was sitting outside on the sill with her legs inside the room – a splendid method, provided she was not afraid of heights, but a painful experience if, as occasionally happened, the sash cord suddenly gave way and the cleaner received a blow across her thighs from the window. By way of adding insult to injury, she was trapped until her screams produced a rescuer.

Monday was entirely devoted to the family wash. Early in the morning, the copper in the back kitchen was filled with soft water and a fire lighted underneath. It was essential to have plenty of hot water at the ready when Mrs Sara Ann Smith, bustled in at eight-thirty. She washed the sheets and other household 'whites' in an oval, galvanized bath set upon a stout wooden stool of the required height. After hand washing, they were transferred to the copper for a regulation boil. While this was going on, Sara Ann washed first the 'coloureds' and then any very soiled or rough cloths, using the same washing water and, when necessary, adding to it. Afterwards she rinsed and wrung and pegged out everything on the long lines that were a permanent feature of the drying-green beyond the back yard. Use of the cumbrous iron mangle was reserved for wet days when the wash had to be dried indoors. Because she knew the strength of Sara Ann's fingers, mother washed the more fragile garments at the sink, and after she had finished, Maud dealt with her own 'smalls'.

Sara Ann twirled a wooden copper-stick to fish out the whites from the boiling water and remembered to add washing blue to the final rinse. Table linen had to be starched: the starch came out of the packet in little white granules – not very easy to mix. When everything was waving in the wind, she returned to the house in triumph: 'All as white as the driven snow!' she would exclaim, as she prepared to wash the kitchen floor with her last pailful of soapy water.

After her departure, it was left to the sun and wind to do their work before the wicker clothes baskets, piled high with dry linen all ready to be folded and ironed, could be brought indoors. In our house, flat-irons were reckoned to be cleaner and more convenient than their predecessor, the box iron. While a flat needed only a place on top of the range in order to heat it, the triangular heater from the inside of a box iron had to be pushed into the middle of a hot fire until it glowed as red as the coals. Although careful manipulation of the tongs was essential, especially during the replacement of the heater in its iron casing, many women said they preferred a box iron because it made a better job of the sheets.

When father kept a couple of house cows, and milk was plentiful, we were able to make our own butter. Bob, the yard man, looked after the cows. He used an outside dairy with a concrete floor and ran all the surplus milk through a separator. The separator was an upright machine of a cheerful red colour; cream spurted from one aperture and skim milk from the other. Every Tuesday morning, the past week's supply of cream was poured into the barrel of a large wooden churn, which revolved in a head-over-heels manner as mother or Maud turned the handle at a steady pace. Now and then, they paused in their labours to peer through a glass eye-hole at the top of the churn in order to assess progress. At last, as if by a miracle, the cream would begin to change its consistency; first, little yellow granules would appear, then, as they increased in solidity, the buttermilk was drained off and the butter scooped out to be washed, salted and slapped up. Like the skim, the buttermilk was fed to the pigs. If my brother or I happened to hear a glad shout of 'The butter's come!', it acted as a signal for us to appear with crusts of home-made bread held out in readiness to receive a dab of the delicious delicacy.

Early on Friday morning, mother began her big bake, with

which she hoped to sustain the household for the greater part of the coming week. Beef patties, fruit tarts, sausage rolls, jam tarts, sponges, buns and Norfolk shortcakes passed in and out of the oven, while Maud, having scrubbed out the scullery and back porch, was waiting her chance to begin work on the outer fringes of the brick floor of the front kitchen. She had to be watched to see that she did not whisk away the cooking-utensils before mother finished with them.

Two or three times a week, the brick hearth in front of the range was whitened with the aid of a preparation known as Paris White. It looked very fine while it lasted. The front door step was treated in the same way, but as children and family were supposed to enter by the back door, the front step remained relatively unsullied, its chalky surface dedicated to the feet of visiting friends and relatives.

It was usual for our one o'clock dinner to begin with meat, potatoes and another vegetable, followed by one of mother's large repertoire of satisfying puddings. The word 'pudding' appeared to imply the use of suet, and butcher's suet, chopped or grated by the housewife, was an indispensable ingredient in its composition. The labour-saving benefits of packet suet were disregarded and the product despised by my mother and her contemporaries as both inferior and extravagant. The flavour of a pudding such as a jam roly poly or a Spotted Dick cooked in a cloth was entirely different from the taste of a similiar mixture steamed or boiled in a basin. A fruit tart or a jam sponge baked in a pie dish was looked upon as quite a light second course, while stewed fruit, baked custard, jelly or a blancmange was reserved for high tea.

At dinner-time, Maud brought in the first course. If it was a roast, father carved her a portion, and she made a bee-line for the kitchen in order to enjoy it before the bell rang for her to remove the used plates and bring in the pudding. Her own table was always covered by a white cloth at meal-times, and everything on it set out very neatly. Mother did not allow slovenliness and would not have been respected had she done so; she also believed in supplying the kitchen in the same way as the dining-room. We all ate the same food, and it was readily accessible. Nothing was locked up except father's drink cupboard.

High tea at five-thirty or six o'clock was our last meal of the day. We ate herring or other kinds of fish, scrambled eggs – occasionally cold ham or tongue. There was a milk pudding and a dish of fruit as well as bread and butter and jam and cake. We had tea to drink, and everything was put on the table at once. Sometimes a child was allowed to have tea in the kitchen, but only when invited by Maud to do so.

Like other farmers of his time, father was extremely conservative in matters of food. If a dish was prepared in a slightly different manner, it at once became an object of deep suspicion. Even a macaroni cheese was unheard-of. Mother would have been more adventurous with her cooking if she had been given the chance. She had family connections further up the north Norfolk coast and sometimes received a bag of cockles or eels or a basket of 'sanfer' from that delectable region. When father was in Norwich, we ate these presents for our Saturday dinner. The sanfer (as it was called) was Marsh Samphire, a species of glasswort, and it was eaten either hot as a vegetable, with melted butter, or cold, after being pickled in vinegar. Either way, one had to scrape or suck the edible surround from the rough inner fibre of the stems.

Saturday was a bread-making day, so dumpling accompanied by gravy or the remains of Friday's stew was a Saturday standby. A true Norfolk dumpling was made with yeast, and a portion of bread dough provided the right mixture. It was put in a buttered and floured cloth and boiled or steamed, and would be eaten with meat or served with jam as a pudding. When it was dished up, the top of a dumpling resembled damp white velvet. Father said that, when he was one of the younger members of a family of ten children and times were hard, he was brought up on bread and milk, porridge and Norfolk dumplings. Should any dumpling be left over at the end of the day, it was fried for breakfast the next morning. The memory of it was too much for him to stomach in later life, so our dumpling intake was restricted to Saturdays only.

'Convenience food' as we know it today was practically non-existent, and the limited range of canned food was expensive and of little importance to country people. We ate everything in its season, and what we could not have, we were prepared to do without. But both the flavour and the food value of the excellent vegetables grown in the gardens of that period were ruined by determined over-cooking. Cabbage, for example, was roughly sliced, placed in a saucepan of cold water and then boiled for an hour before it was considered fit to eat. Although children were constantly told how good cabbage was for their health and general well-being, they hated its smell, its watery appearance and its slimy, undistinguished taste.

Horses working the land

5. *The Farmyard*

A thick privet hedge shielded the paved area outside the back door, but beyond it one moved into the wider spaces of the farmyard. The stables and cart sheds, barns, horse yards and bullock sheds were grouped around the central area and extended along a farm road leading to the stackyard. The farmhouse had its own little yard and outside buildings, including one of the usual cobblestone semi-circular rubbish pits built against a wall, where Maud emptied the tea-leaves and other household debris. The pit was cleared out once a year and its contents carted to the Rookery muckheap.

White House was a farm of less than 200 acres and, as far as I can remember, father kept from six to eight horses, a pony and trap (as well as his car), a couple of house cows, a pen of fattening pigs, a collection of itinerant poultry and a yard full of bullocks during the winter months. In addition, he fattened a smaller number of bullocks in a set of outlying buildings about half a mile from the village near the furthest point of his farm – a common practice, aimed at reducing the time spent in carting roots and straw. Trunch was in a corn-growing area, and local farmers stuck to the Norfolk four-course system of cropping initiated by two great agriculturists, 'Coke of Norfolk' and 'Turnip Townsend', more than a century earlier. Wheat or oats, roots, barley and hay were rotated, in that order. The bulk of the corn was sold to the merchants at Norwich Corn Hall, and the best samples of barley were taken by the maltsters. Bread was a staple food, and beer the favourite drink of the men who worked the land.

The horses the men used were fed on hay and crushed oats; and the horse yards, bullock yards and pig houses were bedded lavishly with straw, which, in its turn, was carted away to manure the fields. The root crop was fed to the bullocks; the pony and cows grazed the pastures, while the pig food included all the surplus milk as well as the contents of the household swill pail. The hens were thrown a daily ration of small wheat or mixed corn, in addition to whatever they could pick up on their peregrinations. Without waste, one product flowed from another to supply a further need, until the annual cycle of the land was complete and the ploughs could again turn over the soil in readiness for a fresh beginning. The concept worked, but the work was hard.

The new age of agriculture came a step nearer when father bought his first tractor. My grandfather (whose farm relied upon horses) viewed the purchase with deep suspicion and took a sardonic pleasure in making a sudden appearance whenever it had one of its frequent breakdowns. Father spent hours tinkering with the tractor's inside and cranking away at the starting-handle. Then young Jimmy, one of his men who had returned after the war, had to be taught to control the new arrival. In 1920, we were on the fringe of modern mechanics, but as yet they had made no great contribution to an older pattern of farm life.

Custom had inured us to the splendour of the horses; and the sight of a plough team against a wintry skyline, or two or three of the huge beasts pulling a painted waggon loaded with hay or sheaves of corn, was so commonplace as to be unremarkable. We did not think it strange that such immense strength should be allied to so much patience and gentleness. Every morning, except Sunday, while we were still in our beds, the oldest horse was left for use in the yard while the rest of them were harnessed and taken to the fields for the day's work. At leaving-off time, the men unhitched any implements that could be left in the field and rode the animals homeward. Carts were backed into the cart lodge below a weather-boarded granary that joined the barn, and later on we would hear the clatter of heavy hooves as the team man (in charge of a stable of horses) headed his troop to the village pond for a leg wash and a drink. I never knew a team man who was not devoted to his horses. He was paid more than the ordinary labourers but had greater responsibility and worked longer hours. 'Them old hosses! He think more on them than he du on his children!' the wife of one of these men used to exclaim.

If the man in charge wanted to turn left, he called out something like 'Kippyah!'; if to the right, the word sounded like 'Wheesh!' A whole vocabulary existed between man and horse, and a good ploughman exerted more control over his animals in this way than he did by using the reins. The team man named his charges, and though there was not a great deal of variation, the names were attractive: Beauty, Boxer, Darling, Lively – often a black horse would be called Prince. When a newcomer of a different breed joined our stable of Shires, it was natural that he should be christened Punch, but the team man maintained that, though a Suffolk Punch had good, clean legs, it did not have quite the same kindly nature as a Shire.

It was a treat as well as an olfactory experience to accompany a man who was taking one of the horses to be shod. The blacksmith's workshop was warm and rather sociable. A few slow Norfolk sentences would be exchanged while the hoof was pared down and the new shoe alternately heated in the fire and hammered on the anvil. Sparks flew out and disappeared into the darkest corners of the smithy. Then there followed the hiss of red-hot iron as it was dipped into a pail of cold water, and an unforgettable acrid smell enveloped us as the shoe was clapped onto the hoof. Nails were hammered in, the blacksmith gave the patient horse a congratulatory slap, and Beauty or Boxer or whoever it might be was led back to the farmyard.

Bob, the yard man, was our link between the house and the farmyard. After the war, he returned to us from Palestine, settled down to courting a nice girl and appeared to have dismissed Gaza from his mind. He was our great friend and ally. Mother made us call the other men 'Mr Brown' or 'Mr Jones', but Bob was never anything but Bob. He was in charge of bullocks, pigs and the animals connected with the house, and during the winter months he had another man to help him with the bullock-feeding.

The bullocks arrived in batches spread over October or early November. They were one of the excitements of autumn. A local dealer bought them for father on Norwich Hill, where pens covered the slopes of the cattle market behind a Norman castle. The market was held every Saturday. We were told that a lot of the bullocks came from Ireland – others from as far away as Canada. They were light or dark red, black or mealy in colour, and when they poured through the gate into their comfortable, straw-covered yard, we thought they must be glad to arrive after such a long journey. It was usual for the bullocks to reach the farm on Sunday morning, after a night spent in a meadow near the dealer's house.

Mr Watts, the dealer, was a stocky, red-faced man who always wore a black bowler hat. When he appeared, driving in a dog-cart behind the bullocks, his son walked in front of the animals to make sure they did not take a wrong turning. The previous day, old Barney, the drover, had brought the beasts out of Norwich market, walking them through the city streets and along sixteen miles of country road before arriving at the meadow. Then, often after dark, Barney walked back to Norwich.

The arrival of the bullocks seemed to bring a new feeling to the farmyard. One sensed that its occupation was complete. They consumed vast quantities of sliced roots – mainly mangolds and swedes – from square wooden troughs. They pulled at hay from racks fixed to the wall of the covered part of the yard. During the last stage of their fattening, they were given a certain amount of cattle-cake which arrived in sacks containing large, brown, biscuit-like slabs – so hard that they needed to be broken up by a special hand mill kept in the granary.

It was interesting to be with Bob in the turnip house while he prepared the roots. Swedes were used first and the mangolds brought into the stackyard to be hodded up; they were piled into a long heap or hod and covered with earth and straw. Mangolds had a sweet, rather peculiar taste, but a slice of swede could be very agreeable. After trimming the roots, Bob threw them into the turnip-slicer, and when he turned the handle, the cut pieces filled his long row of empty skeps, (wicker baskets) one after another. 'Don't go near that machine,' warned my mother. 'One of your uncles lost a finger in a turnip-slicer when he was a boy.'

The bullocks regarded the world outside their yard with a mild, bovine curiosity. Their eyes were large and beautiful, but there was no sparkle in them. If they quarrelled among themselves, it was usually about food. They communicated with each other by snorts and snuffles, and on frosty days their turnip-scented breath steamed upward in the cold air. At night, if you listened at a back window, you were always aware of their presence – the grunts and blowing noises and the rustling sounds they made as they moved about in the straw. My young sister liked to sit on the top of one of the surrounding rails and sing to them; she swore they preferred 'Rock of Ages' to any of her nursery rhymes.

Some of the vets were clever, especially with horses, but in an emergency it was not always easy to get in touch with them quickly enough. I remember a great commotion one morning at home when the yard man discovered a 'blown' bullock. The unfortunate animal was in a bad way, the vet at one of the markets and not available until the afternoon. Father went out of the back door with a determined expression on his face. Some time later he returned and said to mother: 'I'd never had to do it before, and I was afraid I might not hit the right spot. The poor brute was nearly gone, so I knocked the punch through by the rib, and the gas came out like an engine letting off steam!' The bullock recovered.

When spring arrived, the bullocks were sold in small lots, as they became ready for market. All the windows of White House were kept firmly shut while the empty yard was given a final clear-out and the manure carted to the Rookery muckheap, where it was left to mature until the autumn. We accepted the animals' departure as part of farm life and did not mourn. Spring was a time for other interests and occupations.

While they were in leaf, the three horse-chestnut trees standing singly in the Paddock provided shelter from all but the heaviest of rain. The Paddock was just across the road in front of the house, and the chestnuts were the finest trees in it. A continuity of browsing animals had ensured that the outline of their foliage attained an almost semi-circular shape. Towards the end of May, when the weather became warmer and the three trees put up their pale candles of flower, the team man began the summer practice of turning out his horses for the night. It is unlikely that anyone who has seen it will easily forget the sight of carthorses enjoying their first unharnessed outing after a winter spent in stables. The great animals rolled and frolicked like children, then raced about, kicking their heels in full enjoyment of their freedom. After a time they quietened down and began to feed, and within a few days going out to grass became an established routine for the remainder of the summer.

I must have been quite small when I first saw a stallion and his groom on their spring walkabout. We were picking primroses in the lane when a magnificent animal approached us at a slow, proud trot. His mane and tail were beautifully plaited and tied with red and green ribbons, while his coat shone like silk. He looked much bigger than any of the farm horses, and his powerful neck was arched in the manner of a knight's steed in our story-books. The little old groom beside him muttered a 'Good day', and the pair passed on out of sight, a complete mystery, because no one would ever tell us to whom they belonged or where they were going.

Although we were farm-bred children, once away from the hen-egg-chick syndrome we had absolutely no knowledge of the facts of sex or reproduction and were not even aware that such a side of life existed. Even the farm cats gave birth in private, and we accepted the appearance of a young foal or calf without question. We had no inkling of any former connection between a child and its mother, and if we did not believe our aunts' coy references to gooseberry bushes, we were quite content to accept that children came from God.

If a cow produced a bull calf, it was taken away from her, and her forlorn mooing filled the air, but after two or three days she either forgot her loss or became resigned to the parting. The calf was happy enough, though still touchingly young. He settled down in a nice straw-covered loose-box in the pony stable, where he was fed at intervals from a pail of his mother's milk. At first, Bob dipped two fingers in the milk and encouraged the calf to suck from them, but the pretty little creature soon discovered that there was more to be had if he put his nose in the pail.

The gawky appeal of a foal had to be enjoyed from the road – well away from the field gate. I do not think we were tempted to defy father's instructions in order to make its closer acquaintance. A very young foal did not have much control of its legs, and as it grew older, it kicked out in all directions. In addition, the mare was watchful and unlike her usual placid self.

The farmyard hens lived contented lives until they died or a boiling-fowl was wanted in the house. One or two cockerels ran with them and, as the hens laid all over the place, every year a few enterprising birds managed to emerge from secret nesting-places at the head of a family of yellow chicks. This was an exciting event – for children as well as the hens. The birds were captured and confined to a coop for fear of rats, and frequent visits were made to check that all the little balls of yellow fluff were safe and well fed. Once out of the coop, they ran with the other poultry, and the pullets remained to swell the flock; but when the young cockerels began to make fighting nuisances of themselves, they were shut up in separate pens and fattened for the table.

There was always something going on in the farmyard and, more often than not, the big barn was at the centre of it. The front of the barn opened into the yard. One entered by a door near the cart sheds, but, once inside the building, two heavy wooden doors could be unbolted and swung out to give light and to enable a horse and cart to back in for loading and unloading. The dusky interior smelt of sacks and whatever their contents might be. Enormous spiders lurked inside deeply webbed holes at the angles of the walls. Once a year, when the barn was thoroughly swept and cleaned before harvest time, many of the insects were destroyed, but the survivors returned to reconstruct their sinister little dens. When the doors were closed, the only light came from an unglazed opening high up on the west wall, through which owls flew in and out when they were searching for mice. Sometimes a pair of them nested on the sill.

Open stairs near the entrance door led upwards to a granary over the cart sheds, but I do not remember any large amount of corn being stored there. It was upon the floor of the barn that the corn was poured after the filled sacks had been carted away from the threshing-machine in the stackyard. Millions of grains of silky-smooth wheat, rough, prickly barley or pale oats, in shades of gold according to variety, lay piled high behind retaining boards – the fruit of a year's work upon one particular piece of earth. Each grain (as the parson never tired of telling us) was a symbol of resurrection and new life.

After an interval for turning over and drying out, corn which required further cleaning was put through the dresser, a machine rather like a series of sieves which rattled to and fro and made so much noise that it was impossible to hear anyone speak. Two of the men were brought in, father hovered around and all the implements pertaining to the barn were brought into use. With the aid of corn shovels, sack barrows, hand scoops and a brass-bound bushel measure, the grain was sacked up and weighed on the heavy platform scales, and the neck of each sack was carefully tied with binder twine. There was quiet satisfaction all round: another stack or two had been threshed and another part of the harvest stood ready for collection by the miller or corn merchant.

6. *The World of the Fields*

Village children had the freedom of the fields as long as they did not damage growing crops or make holes by worming their way through the hedges. Father's farmland was big enough for our own juvenile explorations, and when we were still at an early age, he taught us how to walk straddle-legged along the rows of a headland in order to avoid treading on the young corn. One of the few times I saw father really angry was when he found my brother and me playing hide-and-seek in and out of the edge of a field of ripe barley. There may not have been much damage done in terms of lost grain, but we soon realized that we had committed one of the worst sins in the agricultural catalogue – almost as bad as smoking or lighting matches near a stack.

A good farmer could read his land like a book and understood its capabilities and limitations. He and his men knew that Nature could make him or break him and that all of them had to live with her. When he was young, a farmer liked to feel that he was as capable of any kind of farm work as the men, because, if he did not fully understand what he was asking them to do, he might lose their respect and, with it, some of his authority.

Each field was known by name and, with its surrounding banks topped by hedges and trees, was as individual as a room in a house. There were differences in soil, size, aspect and shelter, as well as a range of hedgerow vegetation with its related animal and insect population. The trees were mainly oak, ash and holly. Gateways were wide enough to take a horse and cart, and the gates closed in order to keep out cows or any other animals that might be driven along the road. It was usual for farm gates to be bought ready-made, but if a

A harvest rabbit was fit for a king

farmer needed a new gatepost, he felled one of his own trees for the purpose. When the men 'brushed' (thinned out) the hedges, they provided for the future by leaving a strong sapling here and there.

The hedges were largely made up of hawthorn, with patches of blackthorn and myrobalan (cherry-plum), crab-apples, hedge maple and elder. Although local farmers brushed their banks every year during the slack time between haysel and harvest, they preferred to attack the hedges at intervals of some years rather than give them regular attention, and then to use barbed wire to mend the gaps and make weak places stockproof.

The women of the parish were well versed in the culinary aspect of the hedgerows. They knew where to find the best blackberries, and the crab-apples that made the rosiest jelly, and where the sloes and little wild plums grew, as well as elderberries for making wine. A few elderly people gathered certain wild plants to make herbal concoctions, either for themselves or for their animals but, as they seldom divulged the recipes, their secrets were apt to die with them.

Older children had a daily walk to school at either Mundesley or Knapton, but all the youngsters spent a great deal of time outdoors and did not miss much of the life of the banks or ponds and bits of woodland. They saw the annual pageant of wild flowers, beginning with a few sweet violets in February and ending in an autumnal blaze of ragwort and knapweed and scabious. They played games with conkers and acorns, ate hazel and beech nuts and sweet chestnuts and, when they found mallow plants, they searched for the 'pick-cheeses'. Wild strawberries were sweet, but if children knew of a patch of seedling raspberries or gooseberries, they said the birds were always first on the fruit. Girls and boys gathered endless sackfuls of hogweed in order to feed their rabbits, and the boys were particularly knowledgeable about birds' nests and tadpoles.

During April, a great many of the field and roadside banks were yellow with primroses. The village was noted for them. We 'went primrosing' and arrived home with our baskets filled with bunches of the fragile, deliciously scented flowers.

A botanically minded aunt taught us the difference between pin-eyes and thrum-eyes and, like other country children before us, we discovered the little drop of sweetness that could be sucked from the tubular base of the blossom. The pink primroses that grew on one particular bank were despised by our elders as unnatural, but at the same time we were told that, if we found a flower with four petals instead of the usual five, it would bring us great good luck.

As primroses were succeeded by white stitchwort and a mass of red campion, the ferns unrolled their fronds at the bottom of the banks and in the ditches. Grass verges at the sides of the roads were full of clovers and yellow trefoil; later on, they carried hemp agrimony and a selection of hawkbits. In June, the grass on banks and hedgerows rose to its full height; there was a burgeoning of honeysuckle and wild roses, blackberry blossom and, in places, wild hops, with their curious, heady scent. It is easy to understand how, in earlier days, when there must have been so much more of this wild, beautiful, June entanglement, it was natural for our ancestors to accept the presence of a 'Green Man of the Woods' and to carve his face peering through the leaves of some of the medieval stonework in our village churches.

After the hay had been cut, cocked, carted and stacked, work on the farm slackened off until preparations began for the corn harvest. By late June, the nesting season for partridges was over, and the men sharpened their hooks to trim the overgrown banks. When all was shaven and cleared up, the farmer might well feel that for the moment he had the upper hand of Nature.

Village roads were dusty in summer and muddy in winter. When pot-holes became too dangerous, the roadmen filled them with a mixture of stones, gravel and sand, which they firmed with a heavy roller. Stones from one of the local stone pits were heaped at convenient spots by the roadside, and when the village roadman was not otherwise occupied, he could be seen breaking up the larger flints with a heavy-headed little hammer.

On the farm, stone-breaking was an old man's job. As long as a man had any strength left in his arm, he was able to sit on a bank and break stones. Father had a farm road along the side of the Rookery pasture and Levenacre Lane (which gave access to a field of eleven acres) to keep in reasonable condition, as well as the farmyard and its environs. Then there were also farm gateways – apt to become a sea of deep mud during root-carting if not made passable by an occasional load of stones. Mud was one of the problems of rainy weather, and mud-scrapers with long handles were in frequent use. Periodically the mud in yards and on the roads was drawn to the side and, after it had dried out, was either barrowed away or thrown upon the bank.

Field banks provided a living for human as well as animal and insect life. Rabbits were kept in check by a village man who owned a couple of ferrets and a shotgun, while the local rat-catcher did a yearly round of farm buildings and hedgerows. He baited and poisoned, and it was said that he left only enough rats to keep him in a job. The mole-catcher came from further afield; he was a withdrawn, rather unkempt little man who lived alone with two savage old dogs and was reputed to know as much about moles as if he had been one himself. In addition, he worked as a sparrow-catcher. When sparrows became too numerous around the stackyard, he would arrive, lay his corn and finally snare hundreds of unfortunate birds in a large net.

We saw plenty of hedgehogs and occasionally a stoat or a weasel. The villagers told mysterious tales of a second, rarely seen kind of weasel, which they said was very small and extremely ferocious – they called it a miniver, but a visiting naturalist declared it was only the female of the species. Once I saw the pretty sight of a stoat followed by her young running round and round a blackberry bush in the Rookery, and another time came across three or four baby hedgehogs playing like kittens on a footpath where it crossed a cornfield.

Hares were not plentiful, though during the summer you might discover a small leveret crouched in the middle of a field waiting for the doe to feed it. The land around us was not keepered, but it supported partridges and a few pheasants as well as the hedgerow birds. Farmers were not great lovers of birds. My grandfather, who, as a little boy, had spent many hours scaring crows, was positively paranoid about them.

It used to be said that a blind countryman could distinguish the month of the year by the smell of the air. The scent of the fields and woods and the crops in their season was sweet enough, but some of the manure that farmers applied in autumn had a distinctly unpleasant aroma. A pretty red seaweed, which certain tides washed up in great quantities on Mundesley beach, was carted away by farmers and could become fairly pungent in decay; but the worst smell of all arrived with a load of half-rotten herring heads from the fish market at Yarmouth – it might even be a pile of whole fish, when catches were so heavy that the surplus was saleable only as manure. The unlovely mass was spread over a selected field, the local gulls arrived in strength and, until all had been ploughed in, the stench was indescribable.

Farmyard manure was fragrant by comparison. It was said to have a very healthy smell. Bigger and better marrows than those in the garden were grown on the older part of the Rookery muckheap, but they had to be cut and distributed before the manure was carted away to the land in autumn. If stored in a dry place, a fully grown marrow would keep until Christmas.

After harvest, the countryside appeared bare and quiet, although blackberries were still plentiful and the hedgerows aglow with hawthorn berries and rose hips interspersed with poisonous chains of red and black briony. But the fields were no place for small children once ploughing and root-carting and the rest of the autumn work had begun. Swedes and mangolds were pulled by hand, and ploughing went on in all sorts of weather: 'When it is too wet for horses to work, the men can go home' was the rule of the day. Hedges and trees provided shelter, but it was not now so pleasant to sit on a grassy bank and eat the mid-day bread and cheese. Farm-workers wore every kind of old jacket and coat, with heavy leather boots and leggings. On wet days, they added a sack across the shoulders or round the waist – farm sacks and binder twine were put to a variety of uses other than the purpose for which they were intended.

A Norfolk spring can be very cold while the wind is in the east, but if we had the traditional peck of March dust and a few April showers, the fields sprang into urgent life. Partridges called to their mates, and larks sang incessantly above the young corn. Swedes were drilled in flat-topped ridges, giving some of the turnip fields a very neat appearance, and hay scented the air when the grasses began to flower.

Haysel was a June prelude to the August grain harvest. Like most agricultural operations, all went well as long as the weather was kind. The cut grass needed sunshine and breezes to turn it into hay, so the line of grass or swath was 'turned' before being thrown up into cocks. If conditions were suitable, haymaking, like harvest, could go on into the evening, and it was a thirsty time for workers. Cold tea was reckoned to be the most refreshing drink for the field, and old lemonade bottles were used to carry it about. (I do not remember any thermos flasks in 1920.) It was a woman's job to see that her husband had enough drink to last the day, and in hot weather she might have to replenish his supply. All the men used 'frail' baskets to carry their food and drink into the fields: A frail was shaped rather like a present-day, narrow shopping-bag and designed to carry a row of bottles; it was woven of straw or rushes, with a neatly fitting lid and with handles at either side which enabled it to be slung from a horse's harness or from any convenient hook or branch. When men were working late, their wives and children arrived during the afternoon with 'the fourses', a popular break for some hot tea with a meat dumpling or piles of thick jam sandwiches and Norfolk shortcakes.

Towards the end of haysel and again in the harvest field, mother provided a tea for the men. She and Maud worked all morning, baking cakes and cutting bread and butter for ham sandwiches. By four o'clock, the food was placed in a wicker linen-basket, cups packed, all our largest enamel jugs filled with hot tea and the whole lot ready to be carried by hand or pony trap to the hay or harvest field. The men sat amid the hay or on sheaves of corn, while mother and Maud dealt with the tea-cups and we children handed round the food.

When the corn began to change colour, the poppies growing in it burst into bloom. The lighter the land, the more troublesome the poppies. Their seeds were so oily and long-lived that it was impossible for a farmer to eradicate them. The sight was quite breathtaking: every cornfield a harmony of scarlet and dull gold. If the weather was calm and warm, the air became filled with a host of minute black flies which we called midges and which crawled into the crevices of one's clothing. But after a few days the swarms disappeared as suddenly as they had arrived. Farmers waited uneasily: midges were associated with thunder-storms, and at this stage of growth it was not possible for the long straw and heavy ears of corn to right themselves if they were knocked down and twisted by wind and rain. 'The better the crop, the worse it will be laid!' was the usual comment.

Hedging, ditching and root-hoeing were often done by piece-work, and as long as the prospects for getting in the corn were reasonably good, it was usual for the men to agree to 'take the harvest' for a fixed sum. They worked all possible hours, but it was always for the weather to decide if they made good money out of the arrangement or earned little more than their usual wage. On wet mornings, they sat about in the barn, playing Shove Ha'penny, or went home until the day cleared. One year, prolonged rain made a nonsense of harvest agreements and compelled a return to work at normal rates. The ears of corn sprouted green on the sheaves that made up the waterlogged shocks. 'We'll get it, if it takes us until Christmas!' declared my father. But by late September all was gathered in.

There were miserable harvests when the weather was bad, or the crops were light when the price was low; but on the whole, especially from a child's point of view, it was a happy time. Norfolk farm-workers were a good-natured lot and, within reason, we were allowed to slide down a haycock or burrow through a shock of corn without creating ill-will. In addition, there were the thrills of a ride in an empty waggon or even on the back of one of the big horses. But the greatest excitement of all was denied us: only the workers were privileged to enjoy the splendour of a ride on the top of a load.

The youngest member of the harvest work-force was known as 'the holdyer boy'. He was usually about twelve years old, and his application had to be approved by the team man. His main task was to ride or lead the horses while the men pitchforked the sheaves up onto the waggon. The field rang with his shouts of 'Holdyer!' and 'Giddy up!' as he encouraged his charges to move from one shock to another. He was paid the sum of 10 shillings for the duration, and the prestige attached to the job was revealed by the gleam in his eye and the shine on his red cheeks. He walked into the yard with a new assurance: he was the holdyer boy, and a man amongst men.

In general, oats were the earliest grain to ripen, followed by wheat and then barley, but the order depended on weather conditions and the varieties grown. Wheat had the cleanest straw, though its hard stubble was painful to bare legs. Oat straw was softer; barley could be very disagreeable, for the hands (as the men called the awns or barley prickles) stuck to the workers' clothing, travelled up inside their sleeves and could cause intense irritation.

Everyone knew that harvest time had arrived when men with scythes were sent to mow round the headland of the first field. The next day, a horse-drawn cutter-and-binder was able to move in, followed by men who set up the sheaves to dry in the form of shocks – using eight sheaves to make a shock. As the machine was driven round and round, any wildlife that did not have the sense to escape was impelled towards the centre. When a field was thought to contain a number of rabbits, the excitement was tremendous. The harvesters armed themselves with stout sticks, and the inevitable knot of watching children did likewise. My father and the rabbit-catcher appeared, carrying shotguns, and stationed themselves in appropriate positions. The binder continued to cut and rattle out the bound sheaves as the circle of standing corn grew smaller and smaller. When the first rabbit was seen, it was a signal for wild yells and slashing of sticks. It was followed by others. Shots rang out amid shrill cries of 'There he go!' from the younger spectators. Finally the bag was distributed among the men, and everyone calmed down and went home. Harvest rabbits were said to be fit for a king.

After a field had been cleared, women and children were allowed in to glean. They moved systematically over the stubble, gathering the stray ears of corn into their aprons before emptying them into a sack. It was customary that families of those who worked on or had been connected with a particular farm should be the ones to glean there and, when possible, have a share in milk or any other perquisite. Village families made use of the gleanings to feed their hens during the winter, and sometimes they 'shacked out' late-hatched chickens to scrap for the last of the grain and enjoy a few weeks of freedom on the stubbles before the ploughs moved in.

As the corn became ready for carting, one or two outlying stacks were put up, but the wealth of the farm harvest was centred on the stackyard. The stackyard occupied a corner of Home Piece, where the field met the farm buildings. It was a fine sight to see the sheaves pitchforked one by one from the waggon to the elevator and carried upwards to the top of the stack; the men on the stack built it to the ridge and then left the whole ready for thatching.

When thatching had been completed, the great, rectangular shapes of hay, oats, barley and wheat transformed the stackyard. A wheat stack was especially impressive, because the long, strong straw gave it such a solid, Norfolk appearance. A wet season, which encouraged weed growth, made it difficult to dry out the lower half of the sheaves. Should there be any danger of a stack's overheating, a stack iron was laid across the centre during building; part of the iron could be withdrawn from outside, and its temperature gave an indication of conditions within. The remedy for an overheated stack involved complete remaking and was known as 'turning the stack over'. I remember seeing a stack of hay cut open for fear it should catch fire: the centre was so blackened and charred that the hay was useless for fodder.

During autumn and winter, a whole host of small rodents as well as the sparrows arrived to enjoy free board and lodging in and around the stacks. Rats might or might not be a problem, but large quantities of mice were always present. When the bottom of a stack was threshed, it was sometimes impossible to kill enough mice to make any impression upon their numbers. After one particular day's threshing, we saw a large heap of loose straw that literally heaved because of the movement of the mice underneath. All the village cats sat around the straw for days but became so satiated that many of the mice escaped.

Threshing took place at intervals, though higher prices in the spring had to be balanced against loss of grain in stack. When the steam-engine and threshing-tackle rumbled majestically through the farmyard, we knew it was too busy a time for us to be anywhere around; but after threshing was over and the corn safely in the barn, a blind eye would be turned on our exploration of the newly made straw stack. It was an ideal place for a farmer's children to clamber about on, and we grew up with no fear of heights. Mother lived in fear of broken bones, but father said: 'Let them get on with it!'

Gossip after shopping

7. *The Village – Shops and Cottages*

The village had no mansion house and no squire but managed to get along very well without either of them. The absence of an overriding influence may have enhanced local disputes and encouraged a certain jockeying for position at all levels, but it helped to promote individual responsibility. Our way of life imposed considerable social restrictions and apparent class division, yet, no matter how much cap-touching went on, I believe the average labourer was convinced in his heart of hearts that, basically, he was as good as anyone in the land. 'It was a hundred years or so ago,' we were told, 'that the great Coke of Norfolk insisted on wearing his country clothes to attend the King at his Court in London.'

There were little stories always in circulation about condescending Londoners who had been taken down a peg or two by a farm-labourer at work in the fields, and these tales were all the more relished because the holiday-makers were not usually aware of the extent of their undoing – 'He gie me a look and then he didn't say no more!' was the end of the story. A well-known tale concerned a smart townsman who thought he would exercise his city wit upon an old man and a donkey. 'Good morning to you!' said he, as he opened the pasture gate. 'I thought I saw two fools in a field.' But the rustic's face showed no offence. His manner was amiable enough. 'Well, now that make three on us!' he exclaimed.

The rector might have been said to hold the parochial reins, but the village contained a strong chapel element, and he found it necessary to employ even more diplomacy outside church affairs than in dealing with his own congregation. After the rector, our village hierarchy consisted of the occupant of the brewery and the farmers (in order of acreage and ability), one or two middle-aged ladies of independent means, the shopkeepers and the remainder of the parish in order of brains and willingness to assist in parish affairs. If an influential family with a private income had lived among us, it would have ranked with the rectory. No one had ever explained or talked to us about these social differences, but as children we were fully aware of them. We knew that even the hens had a pecking-order. Perhaps, when a way of life has evolved over the centuries from the time of the first settlements in the forests, the participants are inclined to react instinctively rather than articulately towards its more sensitive aspects.

Where the evolution of a village has been based upon agriculture, it seems natural that housing-materials should be shaped by the land and that both land and housing should have considerable influence on the health, appearance and character of the people. By modern standards, the larger houses of the 1920s would be considered cold and comfortless, while the worst of the cottages would be written off as hovels. At the time, older people thought how much the cottages had improved since they were young: they said that thirty of forty years ago circumstances had been such that sometimes whole families died from tuberculosis, one after another, in sad progression. A tiny cottage, an abundance of children, with consequent overcrowding and the land worker's dislike of an open window – even in summer – amounted to a recipe for spreading the disease. Even rich families were not immune, and we were told about the wealthy occupant of the Hall in a neighbouring village, who lost his wife and all his children except one in the same disastrous manner. In 1920, families were not so enormous as they used to be, but we knew one or two old ladies who remembered that they once had fifteen or twenty brothers and sisters – they could not recall the exact number.

The worst of the older cottages had disappeared by 1920, and there was talk of new Council-built homes. Most of the remainder were basically sound and, depending on the landlords, in a fair state of repair. Few of them were owner-occupied. But, whatever its size or state of repair, a house bore the stamp of those who lived in it, and it was people who could make the poorest cottage into a home or turn a much better place into a half-derelict slum.

A minority of the villagers were very simple souls – even simpletons. One or two may have been as twisted in mind as others were in body; many of them were unconquerably obstinate and – given half a chance – incurably argumentative, but almost all of them were hard-working and completely honest. It was said of some of the men that they treated their horses better than they treated their wives, yet on the whole they were kindly, patient folk. 'Hold yew hard!' they would call to an impetuous youngster who was setting too quick a pace in walking or talking, or declare 'That ent roight!' (with a characteristic Norfolk lift of the voice) if a statement was made with which they disagreed. We all shared the same dry sense of humour, and I do not think that any of us were as simple as we may have appeared to be. In fact, whatever the circumstances, we were Norfolk to the bone.

Rheumatism was a great curse of later life. It was popularly known as 'the screws'. One saw old men who were gnarled and twisted like trees, and ancient ladies, bent almost double, with swollen, deformed hands. A cold, damp house, or the mid-day half-hour when labourers in the fields sat on a hedge bank in all weathers to eat their dinner, must have assisted the disease in its painful progress. The better-off were by no means free from it, but their sufferings were alleviated by superior housing and working conditions.

From an early age, I was familiar with some of the cottages. A place of medium size contained a ground-floor front room and a kitchen back room with a large pantry. A door beside one of the chimney-breasts concealed the entrance to a narrow stairway which wound upwards to two bedrooms and, possibly, a tiny third room. Whatever its size, every house had a pantry and, usually, a galvanized meat safe somewhere outside.

Outside there was a separate wash-house with a copper and, round the corner or at the end of the garden, a privy. A sink was a rarity. Water for drinking and cooking had to be carried in pails from the parish pump on the Hill or from a shared well in your own or a neighbour's garden. Its disposal was an easier matter: the housewife either tipped her pail over the iron grating of a street drain or flung its contents upon her own ground.

As in the larger houses, a supply of soft water was immensely important to augment the amount that could be pumped up from the shallow, brick-lined wells. The underlying chalk made well-water hard, so soft rain-water was particularly cherished for washing and cleaning purposes. Rain-water was economical and pleasant to use; it lathered freely with the yellow chunks of household soap and made them last all the longer.

The four cottages in a terrace along the south side of Back Street had no gardens, and their south windows opened onto the churchyard. Each house (one of them had a good, dry cellar) contained a single ground-floor room and two bedrooms above it. The inhabitants considered themselves fortunate because they were allowed to put up their linen lines on a patch of grass across the road. The doors of their privies were numbered and fronted the street adjacent to the end of the terrace; they concealed tiny yards ending in a further door behind which there was a dry closet. A rudimentary night-soil collection was confined to places like this where there was no garden.

It was rare to find a cottage without a piece of land but, in addition, a number of husbands with growing families rented allotments on part of thirty acres of glebe belonging to the church. Aside from the necessity of producing fruit and vegetables, it was important in the economics of cottage life to have outside space on which to hang the weekly wash, and essential to have enough ground for the disposal of the contents of the privy in a decent manner. A privy was always outside the house, and it was routine for the man of the family to empty its contents into holes dug in a certain part of his garden. By reserving a different piece for this purpose each year, a methodical rotation ensured the fertility of his ground. The chore must have been unpleasant, but its reward, in the shape of vegetables, fruit and flowers, was astonishing.

Two or three 'one up and one down' cottages were occupied by elderly widows: the accommodation was sufficient and the workhouse kept at bay, as long as the old ladies remained tolerably healthy or had relatives who could look after them.

The Poor Law Institution was greatly disliked – not least because it represented the death of personal independence. Trunch was in the Erpingham Union, and the workhouse (as it was still called) and meeting-place of the Board of Guardians was situated at West Beckham. As West Beckham was at least ten miles away and not served by the railway, an inmate coming from our parish did not stand much chance of regular visits from either family or friends.

The eastern point of Trunch Hill was occupied by the parish pump and a pond. Two roads met at the crossing on the Hill, and the pond was beside the road to Mundesley. It was really a rain-water drainage pit without any known springs. In normal times, it contained plenty of water and, apart from village usage, served as a horse pond for father's farm. A neatly railed pathway, flanked by a high flint wall, was set well above the water at the back of the pond. The iron railings had become a kind of gymnasium for the village children, whose perilous feats must have tested its strength to the utmost. The possibility of falling into the water or of being dragged away by an irate parent added spice to the somersaults.

The pump stood on higher ground above the hollow of the pond. It had been modernized by replacing a crumbling, circular brick surround and winding gear with a wood-cased hand pump. Most of the houses on the Hill were dependent on this water for drinking and cooking purposes. By day, some of the women could be seen having a gossip round the pump as they drew their water, while in the early morning or evening the men took a turn at the long handle. One or two of the older men suspended their pails from a wooden yoke set across the shoulders.

The gossip of the village women was never ending. It was one of their few recreations. A great deal of it was well spiced with gloom or malice, largely because such additions made the tale more exciting. From woman to woman, it flowed like a tide across the low walls, along the streets and in and out of the shops. Very little went on in the village that was not known and reported in this way, often with so many enlargements and flights of fancy that the original story became unrecognizable. The men were more taciturn. They said they left the clack and the shopping to their wives and daughters.

The village shops were as natural a meeting-place for the women as the pubs on a Saturday night were for the men. It is true that the town of North Walsham was only four miles away, and the excitement of its Thursday market and the lure of the big draper's after-harvest sales attracted custom from all the surrounding villages, but Trunch was large enough to support five shops of its own and, at a time when the majority of people would tell you that they 'used Shanks's pony for getting about', our village shops were relied upon for all the necessities of everyday life. Four of the little businesses stood among the cottages in Front Street, facing the churchyard wall. The owners and their families lived in rooms above and behind the shop, while at the rear they had a stable and outbuildings as well as a long strip of garden.

The outside walls of the post office were panelled with enamel advertising plates, most of them in praise of Mazawattee tea. The name had a fine, foreign sound to it but, perhaps for that reason, we did not see Mazawattee tea in our house. A Mr and Mrs Young presided over the business. Mr Young's silvery beard was always trim, and his wife wore her hair piled high – after the style of Queen Mary. They attended the parish church, and both of them were highly respectable and well-thought-of in the village.

Inside the building, our postal affairs were controlled from a cubby-hole with the appropriate fittings and an aperture through which the penny and halfpenny stamps and postal orders were handed from the inside to the outside counter. Every available foot of wall space was lined with shelves stacked with goods. One large counter dealt with groceries and sweets, while the other overflowed with drapery of all descriptions. Bacon and cheese were kept in an adjoining storeroom, and the paraffin tank was even further away. Whenever the girl who helped in the shop touched the paraffin, she had to wash her hands in a basin of soapy water placed beside the tank for that purpose.

We rarely visited Mr Pike's shop, because he included our house in his weekly round, but as mother believed in buying a little from everyone, we were sometimes able to go further along the street to see Mrs Fuller. At the time, her shop did not appear to be very memorable, but it was the sort of place whose charms were to crystallize into a latter-day nostalgia.

Wherever Mrs Fuller might be in her house or garden, she could not fail to hear the bell attached to the door of her shop. Its penetrating jangle echoed from one end of the street to the other. After the door closed behind you, the shop was inclined to be dim, and the undulations of the worn brick floor could be felt through the soles of your shoes. All the paintwork was very old and had once been a kind of greyish green.

Mrs Fuller was a small, quiet woman who always looked exactly the same. She wore a squarish, grey woollen cap upon her head and was never known to appear without it. I cannot remember ever seeing her on the street. She kept her flour and other bulky commodities in bins or some kind of large container, and the process of weighing it out was always nicely adjusted to the length of whatever conversation was going on. We often bought sugar and would watch while the required weights were placed on the scales. Then Mrs Fuller would wield the tin scoop with slow precision until an exact balance was achieved and she could tip so many pounds of the best 'gran.' into a stiff, blue paper sugar-bag. Following the usual custom, she kept a selection of boiled sweets in large glass jars and made up her sweet bags on the spot. No other shopkeeper could twist a bit of white paper with the same deliberate art as Mrs Fuller. It added considerable dignity to the purchase of a pennyworth of acid drops.

We did not see much of Mr Wegg, the pork butcher, though we enjoyed his famous sausages and pork cheeses. It would be invidious to compare a well-made Norfolk pork cheese with the pallid, glutinous substance called brawn, which one sometimes encountered further afield. The word 'cheese' used in this way appeared to indicate a fairly firm end-product. When fruit such as damsons was cooked, rubbed through a sieve and made into a solid sort of jam that could be cut with a knife, it was known as damson cheese. The bits of meat in a pork cheese were not sieved or minced, but the gristle and bones were removed from the liquid before the final boil-up.

John Spurgeon, family butcher, was as short as his wife was tall. He had a large business and, like all good tradesmen of his time, gave the impression of being a king in his own little kingdom. His house and shop stood at a corner of the Hill, and the shop extended as far as the eastern entrance to the churchyard. The premises behind included a slaughter-house and various sheds as well as stabling for his horse and cart. He had a garden on the other side of the road and hired a small field for pasturing cattle and sheep. The shrill squealing of pigs as they went to their predestined end resounded through the village on certain days, while watching the pigs being killed provided primitive entertainment for such of the older children as were allowed to attend.

Every Friday Mr Spurgeon sent round one of his family to collect orders for Saturday delivery, but on Wednesdays he made a personal appearance, armed with a large, flat basket full of a selection of small cuts suitable for eking out the period between one Sunday joint and the next. The basket was swathed in white cloths and always looked very clean and presentable.

His shop was equally in character. The window was unglazed, with wooden bars and in summer a covering of wire gauze to keep out the flies. A plentiful sprinkling of sawdust on the clean brick floor, and well-scrubbed wooden tables and chopping-blocks in place of the usual shop counter, gave the place an atmosphere all its own. In fact, every one of the village shops was as individual as its proprietor and, to a child's nose, would have been identifiable by reason of scent alone.

8. *Some Aspects of Cottage Life*

The wife of a farm-labourer required considerable stamina in order to cope with the ups and downs of her working day. She had very little money on which to manage, and the bearing of a large family of children and the hazards of illness could bring her to breaking-point. That the majority of these women won through may bear some relation to the training they received during a pre-marriage period of domestic service.

When a girl left school, at the age of fourteen, the usual outlet was for her to go into domestic service. A careful mother placed her daughter as well as she could, according to whatever connections she might have in the world outside her village home. A number of girls went to London – often to families who were regular holiday-makers in the area; or the girls might have a relative who was housekeeper or cook to one of the County families. In a large household, there were said to be opportunities for a youngster to work her way upwards 'behind the green baize door'.

Other women preferred their children to work nearer home. They found places for them in the house of the local doctor, the parson or one of the farmers, and so were able to see their daughters whenever the girls had an afternoon off. Where successful inter-family connections between employer and employee had been established, weaknesses and virtues on both sides were mutually understood and allowed for in all subsequent working relations. 'Sometimes, she du go on at me, but she don't mean nothing,' said a small maid of her mistress; while, 'She's as obstinate as a mule! All the Ts are the same! But she's a good, honest girl at heart,' was the verdict of the mistress upon her maid.

A large saucepan was essential

Wherever a girl was placed, she could expect hard work and plenty of it; but, as long as she was in a decent and well-run house, she received an education in the art of housewifery that would stand her in good stead all her life, enabling her to cope with conditions that would be unthinkable to a young woman of today. When all went well, she remained in her job until she married. In fact, some of the older girls were known to prefer the certainty of a good place in service (especially one with the prospect of an eventual legacy) to the arduous responsibilities of married life. And though some domestic relationships ended in tears and trouble, there were others which resulted in lasting friendships between two different strata of society.

When children left school, it was the girls who were most likely to move away from the village (if the mother was left without the help of her older daughters, their absence meant more room in a crowded cottage), while most of the boys secured jobs in the locality and hoped eventually to settle in their own parish. As a result, in my youth, many families in Trunch bore the same surname, and village relationships – complicated by the occasional illegitimacy – were woven as close as a piece of worsted cloth. The presence of so many Fullers among us was in itself a commemoration of a past connection with the weaving industry. Quite a lot of the men were known chiefly by their nicknames – perhaps, with so little variety in village surnames and such a number of Harrys Toms and Georges, it made for easier identification. The nicknames were highly individual, and most of them bore some reference to a man's youthful likes and dislikes. Three boys in the same family were known as 'Pudding', 'Pie' and 'Tarts', while a fifteen-year-old, who was unable to stop talking about Norwich after his first visit to the city, was labelled 'Norwicher' for the rest of his life.

The cottages that I remember were remarkable for their scrupulous cleanliness. It is true that mother would not have allowed us to visit a dirty house, but such places were very much in the minority. Every year, when spring-cleaning time came round, the ceilings of the pantry and the back room (as the kitchen was called) were whitewashed and the walls repapered. In the older cottages, there were many layers of wallpaper; the occupants claimed that it was the only way to keep the plaster on the walls. Bedrooms received similar attention, and if space was limited as children began to grow up, a bedroom was divided by hangings. Girls on one side, boys on the other was the rule. Downstairs, the window adjacent to the street was veiled in white muslin and its sill occupied by pots of red geraniums.

Because the water-supply was restricted, every soapy pailful of it was used for a variety of purposes, beginning with quite a clean task and ending by washing a floor or a sooty hearth. A woman did all her dirty jobs one after another, before she washed her hands in preparation for cleaner work. On Saturday nights, a copperful of water was heated and the family bathed in succession, using a hip-bath before the back-room fire.

Norfolk farming followed the four-course rotation, and in 1920 women were not encouraged to work on the land. New machinery had supplemented but not displaced the work of men; It left no jobs for the women beyond an occasional 'spudding out' of thistles in the corn. Women worked in the bigger houses, and some of them made a little extra by taking in washing. The majority of cottages had an outside wash-house, with a copper for heating water and boiling the sheets. Baskets of dirty linen were received and returned beautifully washed and ironed for a small charge. A wet day, or a drying-ground at a distance, must have created difficulties, but they were made light of. A cheerful, red-cheeked woman passed our gate on wash-day journeyings between her house and family allotment; she piled her clothes baskets upon an old pram and trundled the lot along at a great pace. 'I'd run a mile to get 'em dry!' she used to declare.

Coal was cheap and plentiful and was the main source of fuel. Many of the back-room fires were in a high grate, others at a lower level, but, whatever its height, the grate had a hob on either side where kettles and saucepans could be placed for long-term simmering. The cast-iron utensils were heavy and soon became blackened by the fire. Considerable ingenuity was needed to cook a family meal with the aid of one large saucepan and, possibly, a smaller pan for potatoes. The housewife would boil a meat pudding for half its cooking time, then surround it by three stone jam jars, two containing vegetables, while the third was occupied by the second course – perhaps a jam rolypoly.

A wall oven was used for the weekly bake: one opened the fire door underneath, lit paper and sticks, then gradually pushed in pieces of coal until the desired temperature was reached. The village women tested the oven with an elbow, because the skin of their hands was too hard to register the heat with any approach to accuracy. Bread and pastries went in first; then, as the fire cooled, buns and sponges were inserted, followed by a dish such as a milk pudding or baked custard which needed a long, slow cook. A nice appreciation of the amount of stoking necessary to produce the required amount of heat was essential, but if all went well, a wall oven was said to bake better bread than a range.

Tea, the biggest meal on five days of the week, was eaten after the men came home from work. On Saturdays they returned at dinner-time. Most of the men had been trained by their mothers or wives to remove muddy boots and leggings, as well as their outer covering of farm coats, in a shed or an outside lean-to before entering the house. (I do not remember any rubber boots at this period.) Occasionally a woman became so inordinately house-proud that, whatever the weather, she required her men folk to strip, wash and put on clean clothes before they were allowed to set foot over the threshold of their home. A giant of a man in a neighbouring village was said to be one of these sufferers. He was the uncomplaining victim of his little wife's mania for cleanliness. One of the highly polished wooden chairs in her back room was upholstered, with a loose cover: gossip had it that, if a visitor so much as sat upon the starched linen, it would be whipped off and into the washtub as soon as the offender had departed.

If a woman of this calibre possessed a front room as well as a back room, it would never be used except after a wedding or a funeral. Her front room would remain completely isolated in the little cottage, like a sort of household god who needed to be propitiated by a weekly offering of furniture polish. Its sedate chairs and tasselled tablecloth would never experience a reasonable usage, while the stiff family photographs and general airlessness combined to make it a place far removed from everyday life.

A cottage wife was often hard put to it if she had to feed a large family. More than sixty-five years on, there are old people living in the villages near the coast who remember days when the price of 'longshore' herring brought to the door varied from sixpence to a shilling for twenty good fish. Their story is always the same: 'Mother gave father two and she would have one, but us children were never allowed more than half a herring apiece!' Other and harsher deprivations may have been forgotten, but the memory of that half herring on a child's plate cannot be eradicated.

A certain amount of pork was eaten, especially when the man was able to keep a pig or two, but very little butcher's meat (as they called beef or mutton), with the exception of a few pennyworth of 'pieces' for soups and stews. Pigs' fry was a favourite delicacy, and some families had a standing weekly order for it. Wild rabbits were cheap and at times given away by the farmers. If chickens were kept, the wife had access to a supply of eggs and an occasional boiling -fowl. Yet, though it was a meat-eating era, those not so well off were obliged to fill the gaps in their menu with a great many vegetables and could hardly be blamed if they considered cabbage and bacon a poor substitute for roast beef.

Baker's bread was good and was bought in large quantities. A man needed half a large loaf, with a hunk of cheese and an onion, to eat in the field during his dinner half-hour. Vivid wartime memories of unpleasant, dusky-looking flour, coupled with a fear of ergot (a poisonous fungus found on rye seeds), made brown bread universally despised, and I do not remember seeing it until the advent of Hovis later in the twenties.

The ubiquitous Norfolk dumpling was regarded as a cheap and universal filler for a growing family. Necessity must have played a major part in the evolution of a dish composed of flour, salt, water and a raising-agent. It was usually served plain, with either gravy or a knob of butter, though sometimes dumplings contained onion, apple or chopped herbs with a little bacon.

A farm-labourer spent a great deal of his scanty leisure at work in the garden. His wife might cultivate a few flowers, but when there was a growing family, it was essential to produce as many vegetables as possible to augment the food supply. The villagers knew nothing of vitamins, but they understood the meaning of an empty belly. Fortunately the soil was a kind one, and the men were expert at getting the best out of their garden or allotment. A good apple tree was a cherished object, and a dual-purpose variety such as a Blenheim Orange provided fruit for both eating and cooking. Applying the principle 'If I can't have it, no one else shall!', it was not unknown for a tenant to cut down a favourite tree before leaving a house to take another job.

When possible, country people liked to save some seed from their own vegetables and flowers. 'Wilson's strain' of onion originated in a little Trunch market garden during the 1880s but, because it was considered to produce top-quality onions, many of the village men perpetuated Wilson's memory year after year by allowing one or two of their finest onions to go to seed. In the 1920s, Wilson's onions were still rated the best. Good Friday was a holiday and a traditional day for planting early potatoes, while St Valentine's Day was said to be the right day to put in shallots. Every good gardener knew the benefit of sowing seeds with the new moon.

Early impressions often last the longest, and I have vivid memories of a few of the cottages and their occupants as they were before or around 1920.

The Gauls were a childless couple who lived in Front Street. Before he retired, old John had been the farm team man, and when I was about five years old, his wife gave my mother occasional help in the house. Sometimes she invited my brother and me to tea. She usually asked us on a Friday, which was her baking day, and collected us from White House for the short walk across the Hill to her cottage.

The way between the Gauls' house and the Pikes' shop was wide enough to take a horse and cart, long strips of garden stretched beyond and a space behind the entrance was partly occupied by a large bullace (wild plum) tree. The fruit was made into a deliciously stiff, yellow confection known as bullace cheese. Mrs Gaul was lucky enough to have a drainage arrangement in the centre of a paved area between her back door and the wash-house, so she did not have to carry pails of dirty water very far to empty them.

After we had turned into her yard and opened the back door and greeted Mr Gaul, we took off our coats and Mrs Gaul tied a large, white starched apron round her waist. Like all the white aprons in our world, it crackled pleasantly if you sat on her lap, but after the initial crackle one sank into it very comfortably. The kettle sang on the hob beside the fire in the high, black-leaded grate, and we settled around the kitchen table for our tea.

There was always a pleasant smell of freshly cooked pastry, and when the pantry door was opened, we could see a wide, well-scrubbed shelf covered with apple pies, a baked custard, a large dish of shortcakes and another of buns. The smell of warm apple, fresh pastry and the tang of nutmeg from the top of the baked custard was very stimulating to juvenile tastebuds. Apple pie and custard were reserved for the Gaul weekend, but we ate home-made kipper or meat paste, bread and butter and jam, followed by buns and shortcakes.

The door between the two ground-floor rooms was kept closed. While the back room was always very neat and friendly, the front room, although equally clean and highly polished, was a little too grand for comfort. I do not think they ever sat in it, nor was the front door ever opened. Unfortunately the way upstairs led from the front room, and the Gauls had to cross its floor in order to reach the staircase door. It must have been a great trial for Mrs Gaul to pollute her front room in this way. I have no doubt that she laid newspapers over the carpet before she and her husband went up to bed.

My only recollections of the conversation on these

occasions is of old John's evident disapproval of anything to do with Women's Suffrage and the Pankhurst family. 'If you don't behave yourself,' he would say, 'that there Mrs Pankhurst will come down the chimney behind me and carry you off!' For years, I thought the lady was a particularly loathesome kind of witch and was determined not to be taken for a ride on her broomstick.

Sara Ann Smith, already encountered as our washerwoman and as the mother of our young maid, lived in one of the terraced cottages on Back Street. She was a middle-aged, squarely built woman who took life in her stride and, in so doing, extracted every ounce of enjoyment from it. When I first remember her, she had reared eight children of her own, plus a grandchild or two. Her husband was a small man whose Christian name we never heard, because Sara Ann referred to him always as 'Smith'. Over the years, there were few births or deaths in the village at which she was not present. She seemed to be either helping people into life or attending them on the way out of it. She nursed sick neighbours with impartiality, and when she took over the weekly wash at our house, she very much enjoyed telling mother all about her experiences.

When old Mrs Baker in the Back Street had a stroke and was bedridden for two years before her death, Sara Ann looked in every day and did things for the invalid of which her husband was incapable. We were told: 'Sometimes she look at you very funny indeed, and all she ever say is "Oh dear! Oh dear!" ' One day I was allowed to accompany Sara Ann and was able to verify her story.

Mrs Baker's bed was in the living-room, and her husband sat in a chair before the fire, which was in the usual high grate. She was very clean and her hair was neatly combed, but her face looked rather strange. When I took her limp hand, she said 'Oh dear! Oh dear!' without any change of expression.

Sara Ann gazed at the still form with considerable pride, rather in the manner of a museum curator showing off his prize exhibit: 'Well, there you are, Miss! Every day I wash her and rub her back and bring her a little bit of something like a baked custard – because Baker's no great cook – and "Oh dear! Oh dear!" is all she ever say to me. The nurse come once a week and she say I can't do no more.'

Two large china cats on the mantelpiece appeared to watch over old Mrs Boulter as she sat beside the bright fire in a cottage on the Hill. Her white hair was scraped up to the top of her head in a tight little knot, and her daughter hovered protectively in the background. Mrs Boulter produced a biscuit from a special tin she kept in the wall cupboard, and told me the story of the day she nearly died.

'I was always sickly as a girl,' she said, 'but when I turned eighteeen, I was that bad my relations all come to look at me, and when they had seen me they walked to Walsham and bought their blacks for my funeral. But I did 'em all, Miss! They bought their blacks for nothing. I did 'em all proper, for I got well and married Tom and had Polly here!' Her little, dark eyes twinkled, and one imagined the relatives slinking off like so many crows disappointed of the funeral feast. 'Now, I fare to be eighty year old come Michaelmas,' she continued chattily, 'and I'm ready to go when the Good Lord want me.'

9. *The Church and the Village*

For hundreds of years, the church of St Botolph had been the centre of the village in a material as well as a spiritual sense. A fourteenth- and fifteenth-century rebuilding superseded the earlier church, whose origins may have stretched beyond Domesday into years when the teachings of St Botolph were radiating from Iken – a remote and lovely corner of Suffolk where the saint is said to have landed in 647. Trunch church was enriched by some of the wealth of the wool trade, and it survived the organized vandalism that followed the Reformation and all the changes during and after the Protectorate. It played its part in the joys and sorrows of generations of villagers, was hallowed by their prayers and, when they died, witnessed their burial in the surrounding churchyard.

It was not difficult for a village child to accept the parish church as 'God's House'. It appeared logical that a Being as great and wonderful as God should have a large and splendid house which His people could care for and where they met together to worship Him. 'He is there,' we were told, 'but you cannot see Him.'

Two chapels as well as a large parish church in a village with a population of fewer than 400 souls created rivalry and occasional backbiting, yet gave a lot of people a chance to organize religious activity or serve their own church in a way that might not have been open to them had they remained in the Church of England. Although church and chapel had their own distinctive ways of worship, there was always a certain amount of give and take between them. When a Methodist farmer married a Church of England girl, they solved their denominational problems by attending chapel in

Font and canopy, Trunch church

the morning and church at Evensong. All burials continued to be in the churchyard, because the chapels had no burial grounds – 'We'll all be the same on Judgement Day!' was the usual comment.

When a memorial to commemorate the men of the parish who had fallen in the Great War was erected in the churchyard, the whole village contributed to its cost and attended the dedication and subsequent Remembrance services. As long as a rector understood his people enough to avoid shattering the delicate balance of parochial religion, any disputes between church and chapel were seen in their true perspective and did no real harm.

The rector was constantly about the village. He knew the people in their homes as well as in the street. He had to be a bit of a diplomat as well as a priest, and in his darker moments he must have thought of his parishioners collectively as an obstinate, self-opinionated, troublesome lot. He was looked up to as the top man in the parish and was expected to predominate in village affairs as well as those of the church. The influence and example of the rector and his family set the tone of a parish during his incumbency, though perhaps the worth of a good parson was never fully appreciated until after his departure, when, under a different regime, the villagers began to sigh for the old days and talk longingly of 'what we did in Mr Y's time'.

In 1832, the living was held by a scholarly man who needed a larger house to accommodate his students. He decided to demolish the existing rectory near the tithe barn and build a new one on adjacent glebe. Professor Jarrett's enormous kitchen, said to have been his students' common room, was used by our rector and his wife for all church and village meetings not considered large enough to be held in the parish hall. In 1920, the rectory garden, surrounded by glebe (part of which was let for allotments), was in demand for summer fêtes, missionary meetings and other outside events. The rector was president of the men's bowls club, and the lawn in front of his house was used as the club green. His wife ran the Mothers' Union and the Sunday School. A wide cross-section of the village was familiar with the house and garden and knew that the rector's study door was always open if help or advice were required.

Once or twice a year the church-going members of the village renewed their zeal for the work of Missions to India. A missionary and his wife on home leave were asked to spend a weekend at the rectory; on Friday night the missionary gave a lantern lecture in the parish hall, and on Sunday he preached at Matins and Evensong. The congregation prayed for the success of his mission station and sang 'The heathen, in his blindness, bows down to wood and stone' with considerable fervour. Church collections were sent to the mission, and in July or August it was aided by a sale of work held on the rectory lawn. One stall was devoted to an assortment of brilliantly coloured handkerchiefs and gauzy scarves, little animals carved from foreign woods and some beautifully embroidered traycloths and afternoon teaclothes produced by the Indian girls at the mission school.

We did not go to Sunday School but were taken by our parents to church for eleven o'clock Matins. When the bells began to peal 'Come to church! Come to church!' at ten-thirty, we got into our Sunday best, complete with hats, gloves and clean handkerchiefs, and twenty minutes later we set off past the village pond, across the Hill and along the short stretch of path between the butcher's shop and the Crown Inn towards the churchyard gate. The practice of renting pews had been done away with years ago, but it was customary for certain pews to be associated with each of the larger houses, and no one other than the usual occupants would have dreamed of sitting in them.

Inside the church, one of the churchwardens or a sidesman preceded mother up the aisle and opened the door of the White House pew for her. The greater part of the congregation were shown to their seats in this way and, though formal, it was friendly because of the smiles and familiar faces. My grandmother and aunts sat in the Ivy House pew, but grandfather preferred a back seat near the south door which he had occupied as a boy and young man, when he lived with his old granny. The wardens and sidesmen were elected at an annual general meeting. The rector nominated the senior, or rector's warden, while the office of people's warden was left to the choice of the parish. In practice, the rector chose his warden from among the more influential parishioners, and the people elected a well-respected churchman from a slightly lower walk in life. Both men had considerable influence, took their responsibilities very seriously and could be re-elected year after year.

The time taken by the morning service varied from between 1¼ and 1¾ hours, and the rector had the assistance of a good choir, plus a wife who played the harmonium. Small children were often taken out before the sermon. A service of Holy Communion was incorporated with Matins on one Sunday a month and the Litany on another. The second part of Holy Communion was taken after the final hymn and a brief interval, during which all the children and non-communicants left for home. A lot of the cottage families preferred to attend Evensong. The men segregated themselves in the north aisle, while their womenfolk found seats elsewhere. The same custom was observed in the morning but was not so noticeable because fewer men were at church.

Although the church was surrounded by houses, there were no complaints about the sound of the bells. They were rung for Sunday services, weddings and funerals and to mark the occasion of a death. While the passing bell tolled the age of the deceased, those within earshot would say: 'That'll be old John S' (or whoever the sick one might have been), and for a little time they would talk about John and his family. If the illness had been a long one, it was usual to agree that the end had come as 'a happy release'. The smallest bell was rung only on the death of a child. In our garden, its thin, slightly cracked note sounded through the autumn air. Mother stopped picking apples while she counted up to nine: 'It's poor little Mary F,' she said, and for the first time in my short life I was acutely conscious of my own mortality.

Our area of Norfolk was uncompromisingly Protestant. My grandfather could remember his parents talking of the days when effigies of the Pope were burned instead of Guy Fawkes on 5 November. When, at the age of forty, one of my great-aunts decided to turn Roman Catholic, her family refused to speak to her and although she had been in the habit of paying regular visits to her brother, my grandfather, it was twenty years before she was again asked to his house. As with other matters of which they disapproved, the Church of Rome was simply not spoken of either in our family or in the village. They ignored ritualistic traces of the pre-Reformation era in their parish church as if such reminders did not exist. For years, I thought features such as piscina niches and holy water stoups were religious kinds of receptacle for arrangements of flowers and vegetables at certain times of the year.

Trunch church was decorated for Christmas, Easter and Harvest. A number of the female members of church-going families took part in the work, from the rector's wife up in the chancel to the Sunday School children who, at Easter, collected quantities of primroses and moss to ornament the nave windowsills. Once a family had been asked and had undertaken to decorate a particular part of the church, the task appeared to become theirs by right – to be relinquished only in face of death or disability. The rector's wife took charge of the operations with commendable caution, and the rector looked in at intervals to admire the decorations and encourage the decorators.

My aunts were kind enough to allow me to help while they 'did' the screen. The task occupied us most of the day, in addition to time spent in gathering the appropriate flowers and greenery. Whatever the season, the preliminary work involved a number of jamjars and cone-shaped containers, all of which had to be positioned with the aid of a great deal of string.

At Christmas, the beautiful building was resplendent with holly and evergreens. My aunts made long ropes of ivy and berried holly which they ran along the middle rail and base of the screen and up the muntins (vertical posts) as far as they were able to reach. By the time the precious Christmas chrysanthemums were arranged in their receptacles, we were quite exhausted, but happy to remain for a while to admire the rest of the church and to receive the congratulations of our fellow workers or anyone else who might drop in to have a look at the final result.

On Christmas Eve members of the choir started carol

singing at 11 p.m. As they began their rounds by visiting outlying parts of the parish, it was often 3 a.m. before we woke up to 'Hark the herald angels sing!' It was a dream-like experience to hear through frosty dark in the earliest hours of Christmas morning. Eight hours later, the choir was in its usual place in the chancel, surrounded by holly and ivy, and it was Boxing Day before the carol singers' collection tin was brought to our door.

The orchard at Ivy House was full of bulbs, and every spring it was feared that either the daffodils would not be out or the flowers would be over at the time they were wanted for the church. But the season seemed able to adapt to a moveable Easter, and we always had daffodils, though occasionally my aunts were obliged to gather them a few days early and stand pailfuls of buds in the scullery to encourage them to open.

The old screen looked very lovely at Easter. Long trails of smilax and an abundance of daffodils made it a memorable picture. All the same, I do not think that my relations or any of the other decorators valued the screen or the font for the precious objects they were, but looked upon them as merely a base for their floral offerings. Once or twice, I remember a portion of one of the crockets on the upper part of the screen rattled to the floor while the smilax was being arranged: 'This wood is becoming quite rotten,' remarked my aunt, as she swept up the medieval fragments into her dustpan.

In a village where everyone was dependent upon agriculture, the annual Harvest Thanksgiving was a very personal occasion, and it strengthened the link between the church and the land. It would have been unthinkable to hold the service before the last of the corn was in stack. We decorated the screen with red dahlias and little bunches of oats, a sheaf of wheat was placed at either side of the chancel archway, and apples, carrots and cabbages were piled on the floor like offerings laid at the feet of the painted saints above them. Almost every man in Trunch was a good gardener, and nothing but the best of their fruit and vegetables was sent to church or chapel: the entire church glowed with the fruits of the earth; it smelt delicious, and the giant marrows in their customary place beside the font seemed to become larger every year.

There was a feeling of earthy satisfaction about Harvest Thanksgiving that was absent from the more sacred services of Christmas and Easter. The village people sang the familiar hymns with the results of their labours all about them. To roar out 'All is safely gathered in' was as meaningful as to hear the parson read 'By the sweat of thy brow shalt thou eat bread.' Thanks to an established religious training in church or chapel, all those who could read were familiar with the Bible. That is not to say that they necessarily followed its teaching, but whatever they might or might not get up to, at least they knew the difference between right and wrong.

Local clergy often exchanged pulpits for the harvest services. The rector of a village about three miles away was a popular visitor, and his sermon was eagerly awaited. He was a well-known horseman and famous for his down-to-earth attitude to life. 'When I hear Reverend B start on about muck,' said an old man who sat in the north aisle, 'I know he'll say suffin' I fare to understand.'

Throughout the village, Sunday was looked upon as a day that was different, though it was observed more strictly by the old than by the young. In 1920, grandfather would not play a game of bowls or allow a Sunday paper in his house, but father took a Sunday paper and saw no harm in a family game of bowls as long as it took place on his own green. As children, we were allowed certain toys and books which were kept in the Sunday cupboard but were not forbidden our usual playthings.

The yard man and the team man came in to look after their animals, but no other farm work took place on Sunday, even during the more urgent periods of haysel and harvest. If a little gentle gardening was attempted, the man with a hoe in his hand might be heard to say – in half-defiant self-justification: 'Well, what I say is "The better the day, the better the deed." ' Sunday was the day for a family afternoon or evening stroll, when the village men took a quiet look at other fields, comparing the crops with those on the farms where they themselves worked. Farmers had a walk round their own land, making tentative plans for next week's work, while fully aware that any change of weather might cause a complete turnabout of the arrangements.

Sunday tea was a time to entertain one's family and friends. Summer and winter alike, my parents and their children walked along the road to Ivy House to have five o'clock tea with my grandparents and aunts. The bread and butter was cut wafer-thin and the long dining-table covered with various kinds of cake, little dishes of jam and a banana jelly. When the meal was over, we were allowed to open the Ivy House toy cupboard, where, among other things, I remember a splendid *Book of Cats* illustrated by Louis Wain, and other little books which contained more up-to-date pictures by Mabel Lucie Attwell.

A few of the village children were known to belong to both church and chapel Sunday Schools – thinking it worth while, because then they would have two Sunday School Treats instead of one. I do not know what arrangements were made for the chapel children, but for a time the Church Treat was held at Gunton Park, an estate about six or seven miles away, which belonged to Lord Suffield. The better-off church-goers gave donations, and farmers took it in turns to provide transport. The horses and waggons were decked out for the occasion with flags, ribbons and bells, and children, Sunday School teachers and an extra helper or two made the journey in considerable style. The rector, his wife and the oldest teacher travelled more sedately by car. Parents and well-wishers gathered at the school corner to give them a good send-off, and their final admonitions and 'Hip, hip, hoorays' were answered by a farewell burst of flag-waving before the waggons trundled out of sight. The children sang all the way to Gunton. A day's programme of games and sports was laid on, and I think they took a picnic lunch and followed it with a tea provided by Lord and Lady Suffield. At dusk, the waggons returned, the younger children half asleep, while their sisters and brothers continued to sing the well-known songs in shrill little voices, hoarse with fatigue. It was a great day.

A game of bowls

10. *The Sociable Side of Life*

The cottages did not often entertain friends or relatives, but when they did, it was an event known as 'having company'. If a woman said she would be unable to work on a certain day because she was having company, her employer knew better than to argue.

Farmers' wives and children had little time or opportunity for an organized social life. We heard mother speak of having gone to Norwich dances and concerts before her marriage but, as father was not musical and did not dance, she had to adapt herself to the situation, although she insisted on taking us to the theatre to hear some Gilbert & Sullivan when the D'Oyly Carte Company made its annual visit to the city. Mother did not encourage us to mix with the village children, taking the view that we must play with all or with none of them. She did not wish us to play with them all, so rather than create any bad feeling we had to remain aloof. We learned to develop our own interests and did not find it difficult to do so, but I had no real friends of my own age until I was sent away to school.

Mother's only formal entertaining was an occasional four o'clock tea-party in the drawing-room. It was usually a ladies' affair. The best china and silver were very much in evidence, and Maud wore her laciest cap and apron with a black dress as she opened the front door to guests and brought in the tea things. We children were expected to behave ourselves and help to hand round the bread and butter, tiny sandwiches and several different kinds of cake; but, after such a display of good manners, it was always a relief to give a hearty tug at the bell rope when mother asked one of us to ring for some more milk.

The practice of paying afternoon calls was losing ground. When making a formal call, it was the correct procedure for a married women to present three cards – one of her own and two of her husband's when he was absent. The conversation was uninteresting and mercifully short-lived, because the accepted duration of a call was about fifteen to twenty minutes. Mother's tortoiseshell cardcase was seldom in use, except when the village had a new rector or there was a change at the Brewery House: she said she had no time to go out of the village and that my aunts could do all the calling further afield; but she continued to keep a card tray on the hall table, even if Maud did not often get the opportunity to present it.

The majority of our visitors were friends or relatives who dropped in for a chat, though, more rarely, guests arrived to stay for a few days. The ladies were never idle: they walked about the house, busily crocheting away at a strip of lace edging which lengthened visibly as it dangled through their fingers. During the evening, they sat with mother, sewing or knitting while they exchanged a stream of news, mutual reminiscences and the kind of genealogical conversation that began in this fashion: 'Well, she was a T, wasn't she? They were always a difficult family. Her mother had six children and came from …' This sort of talk was of perennial interest and went on in any kind of household. It ensured that, as well as discovering most of the ramifications of one's own and the other farming families in the neighbourhood, at village level, the whole population knew a great deal about each other's ancestors. It was not always necessary to have personal contacts with a family in order to take an interest in it. My aunts and great-aunts, in company with others of their age, knew quite a lot about some of the aristocracy and even more about the royal family. It was a point of honour with them to be able to answer any question on the subject of Queen Victoria's children, their marriages and their descendants. As far as my aunts were concerned, life began with Victoria, and I do not remember hearing them mention earlier sovereigns.

Before visitors came to stay, mother had a ham brought down from the attic. It was boiled and served cold at high tea, but otherwise she did not produce any special dishes. To serve wine with a meal was looked upon as the act of a spendthrift and, like all such extravagances, was said to result in bankruptcy. Farmers told each other that to drink beer and whisky was good for the barley trade. Father's beer was delivered from Trunch brewery, but his whisky arrived from Scotland in a stoneware jar that could be fitted with a tap. I have a 1931 receipt in which a two gallon jar of best Scotch whisky was charged at £7.10s.0d., carriage paid by rail from Glasgow, with a refund of 5s.6d. on the container. It cost less in 1920. Even so, beer and whisky were drunk very sparingly in our house, and two or three bottles of homemade sloe gin in the drink cupboard as well as the bottle of port and another of brandy were reserved for illness or very special occasions.

After the war, father turned a piece of his garden into a bowling-green, and the less strenuous periods of summer were punctuated by bowls parties. At one time or another, the majority of the men in the neighbourhood must have had a game of bowls on father's green. We used to watch, fascinated, not by the play, which we did not understand, but by the varying antics and attitudes of the players as they sent up the jack and stooped to bowl. Some of them ran the length of the green alongside the wood as if their excited gestures could coax it into a different path. During the winter, father had a weekly card night when he and three or four friends visited each others' houses for a game of Solo. The wife of the host brought in coffee and sandwiches at half time, made a little social conversation and vanished when play resumed.

Croquet was a great summer pastime for the whole family. If you possessed a lawn and a croquet set, you became hooked. Mother and my aunts played with us, and sometimes father and an uncle could be persuaded to join in. When other children came to tea, we played incessantly and discovered, through bitter experience, that, unless we were able to control our frustrations and tantrums at the pangs of being 'croqueted' out of a promising position, we were simply no good at the game.

Children were encouraged to play all sorts of card and

other table games during winter evenings and on rainy days. Our parents taught us how and then left us to get on with it. We passed hours and hours with board-games such as snakes and ladders, ludo, halma and draughts, as well as dealing the cards for Happy Families, Old Maid, Snap, Cheat and an interminable game called Draw the Well Dry. We learned to play the simpler varieties of Patience, and when we reached the age of nine or ten, we were taught whist. At Christmas time, we were generally asked to one or two children's parties, where, as we grew older, the games progressed from Ring o' Roses and Hunt the Thimble through Postman's Knock and How Green You Are to the relative sophistication of Musical Chairs and Sir Roger de Coverley.

When not occupied by corn, the barn was a splendid place to play in during wet weather. Our two swings hung from the crossbeams, and there was plenty of room for ball games. On better days, we were fond of clambering about in the stick house, or daring each other to walk along and sometimes to jump from the top of the garden walls. Encouraged by our botanical aunt, we made collections of pressed flowers, birds' eggs, butterflies and moths, and filched mother's two-pound glass jamjars to house a little menagerie of caterpillars which we fed with suitable leaves and cleaned out daily. One was on close terms with a caterpillar in a jamjar. If it lived long enough to pupate, it might live still longer, to make a safe emergence in its final form. It was fascinating to watch an insect's shrivelled wings expend into the glory of a Red Admiral butterfly or one of the Hawk moths.

The aunts drove a pony and trap and sometimes took us to the beach, but when father replaced his big pony and dogcart with a smaller animal and a governess cart, an afternoon on the beach played a more regular part in summer outings. Jenny was harnessed, mother took the reins, we packed into the trap with our spades and buckets, and Jenny set off for Mundesley, two miles away along the dusty road. She took her time over the outward journey but sped homeward as fast as mother would allow her to go. At Mundesley we stabled her at the Ship Inn, where a steep, cobbled gangway led down to the beach. The landlord stood at the inn doorway while the ostler unharnessed the pony; he was an extremely stout, Humpty-Dumpty of a man, whose arms and legs appeared out of all proportion as they emerged from his enormous egg-shaped body.

The old-style bathing-huts on wheels were drawn up on the sandy beach near the promenade; they were no longer horse-drawn to the sea. One of my aunts liked to bathe, so she hired a hut in which to change into her navy serge bathing-dress with red braid round its neck and short sleeves; daringly, the legs of the costume ended just below and the short skirt just above her knees.

With her usual suspicion of strangers, mother did not encourage friendships with the summer visitors who took rooms or stayed at Mundesley hotels and boarding-houses during the school holidays, but sometimes she let us join in a service conducted by the Children's Special Service Mission. The CSSM was run by groups of theological students and their helpers. During August, they organized a programme of beach games, competitions and religious services for children at the seaside towns and larger coastal villages. For those who went to the beach every day, it must have been fun. I think we enjoyed the services, but memory of them has crystallized into a picture of sitting on the sand among a large circle of children while an earnest young man with curly hair and a striped blazer led us in a song which began 'Joy, joy, joy, with joy my heart is ringing!'

A farmer's business activities kept him in touch with his fellows. Father's friends were fond of a game of cards and, after a Thursday market in North Walsham or the Saturday market at Norwich, they often spent the remainer of the afternoon playing Solo. In a business sense, Norwich was the agricultural heart of the greater part of Norfolk, and Saturdays saw the city taken over by the country. Cattle were driven through certain streets to and from the market-place, and it was not unknown for an alarmed shopkeeper to be confronted by an inquisitive beast on the other side of the counter. Farmers met on the Cattle Market or in the Corn Hall, while their wives shopped, met relatives or friends and recognized acquaintances all along the street. Many of the farmers went to Langfords or the Red House for coffee or lunch, but their wives and children were to be found at the Corner House or Princes in Castle Street.

Mother did not always accompany father to Norwich, but when she did, she usually went to Princes. The room was very light and bright inside, but private, because green curtains screened the lower parts of the windows from the street. The proprietress, a Mrs Pillow, sat at a desk just inside the door; she had a straight back and an imposing hairstyle, and was obviously not a woman to be trifled with. Mrs Pillow knew each of her established customers by name and exchanged little bows and greetings with them as they entered. Occasionally a newcomer would sneak in and sit alone, as if ostracized. It took time to become fully accepted at Princes.

Very rarely, if mother decided we needed more to sustain us than soup or a beef patty, we were taken to Buntings, where there was a restaurant on the top floor of a large clothing store. Palm trees in large, shiny pots stood all over the place and, shaded by their greenery, we ate a meal of three courses – soup (tomato or Brown Windsor), meat and two vegetables, followed by a pudding. I think the cost was 1s.3d. for an adult and 9d for children.

Once they were sensible enough to be trusted not to venture into the streets at either end, it was considered quite safe to leave children to their own devices for half an hour in the Royal Arcade while mothers went about their own business. The arcade was weather-proof and traffic-free and, among other attactions, it contained a first-class toy shop. When mother returned, she took us to Shapleys, where she bought a pound of special sweets, asking for them to be sent to the garage where father parked his car. It was never necessary to carry parcels about Norwich as long as one was able to pick them up at some central point. All the better shops employed messenger boys with bicycles, and we knew that our box of sweets would be neatly encased in brown paper, tied with white string and delivered at Mann Egertons before five o'clock.

If one excluded a minority who liked to keep themselves to

themselves, most of the inhabitants of Trunch were willing enough, and the better-off sufficiently public-spirited, to ensure that some kind of social entertainment was provided for everyone.

Very little cricket was played in our area, but bowls was a game popular among men in every walk of life. The village men ran their own bowls club, with the rector as president, and played on the rectory lawn one or two evenings a week throughout the summer. When father's new green became playable, he held an annual bowls party for the men who worked on White House and Ivy House farms. Socially, the men were quite well provided for. After the end of the bowling season, Men's Club nights began at the village hall. On those evenings members could play billiards or darts or have a game of draughts or dominoes and a chat beside the fire without the expense of going to the pub for a drink.

The rector's wife organized the Mothers' Union, and I think there was a Girls' Friendly Society. Mother belonged to the MU, though she was not always able to go to meetings, and occasionally she held a tea party for members. One of the things about which mother was emphatic was (as she said), 'When you give the village women a formal invitation to tea, you must have it in the drawing-room and use the best silver and china as well as giving them nice food.' She said that was what they enjoyed and expected.

The village hall was used for a variety of purposes. It was a large place, with a stage and a small kitchen; when it was built, toilet facilities were not considered a necessity, presumably because the hall was surrounded by fields. We did not go to the two or three parish socials held during the winter but were often taken to fund-raising events. When there was a lecture or concert, the hall was filled with chairs and long benches – some of them brought from the school. Mother or one of the aunts accompanied us, and we had to sit at the front near the platform. Naturally we would have preferred to be at the other end of the hall and cat-call with the back-benchers.

Lantern lectures were about either travel or missionaries, and though pictures of foreign lands and faces were interesting, a long-winded lecture on them could be dull for children. It was the handling of the lantern that provided our chief amusement – especially if the speaker was more accustomed to talking than to manipulating the slides. When he inserted them upside down, many of his audience groaned in a full-blooded way, then cheered when at last he got it right. Sometimes the lantern went out, and everyone was obliged to sit more or less in darkness while the lecturer fiddled about with a torch and the rector wondered if the hanging paraffin lamps should be relighted.

A village concert was not entirely a musical evening. Songs and piano-playing were interspersed with recitations and dramatic sketches. A parish group gave a show of that kind in the autumn and spring of each year. The concerts were in aid of village hall funds, and the group devoted many of their evenings to rehearsals. When the great night arrived, the place was packed out.

More rarely, a party from outside the parish put on a show in aid of a local cause, giving a performance in every village that was likely to benefit when the desired object was achieved. About 1920, plans were afoot to build a cottage hospital in North Walsham, to serve the town and surrounding district. A tremendous effort was being made to boost the fund and, among other projects, a concert party was formed to give performances throughout the area, with the aim of stimulating interest as well as raising some of the necessary money.

One of the most popular members of the party was a North Walsham draper who had a pleasant baritone voice. He was never allowed to leave the platform until he had given us a song called 'Mary Ann, she's arter me!' The village knew most of it by heart: they bawled out the chorus, 'For she want me for her young man!', and demanded as many encores as the singer was willing to give. Another individual specialized in broad Norfolk stories, and his tale about the owner of a sick donkey was a perennial favourite. When the man went to a vet for advice, he was given a powder with minute instructions as to its adminstration to 'th' owd dicka'. He was to place the powder in a piece of rolled-up paper, persuade the donkey to open its mouth and then blow the powder down the animal's throat. The audience chuckled its way through the preliminaries, and everyone knew what had happened next, when, on the following morning, the vet encountered the owner, who looked in very poor shape. Yet there was always the same tense pause while the vet made his enquiries, followed by peal after peal of laughter at the unhappy man's reply: 'That worn't no good, marster,' he said. 'Yew see, that owd dicka blew fust!'

The church fête was the most important of the annual events held on the rectory lawn. The delicate sensibilities of the lady helpers were the biggest impediment to its success. But once the participants had been fitted into place without undue outrage to their feelings, preparations could go ahead, and the organizers knew that, unless it rained, all would be well on the day. The stalls and side-shows were placed round and about the main lawn, while tea could be taken at little tables placed on the grass near the kitchen window. Cups of tea and plates of home-made scones and cakes were handed over the sill to the teenaged waitresses, who supplied the customers and received their money. The most popular attraction was bowling for a pig, and its presence guaranteed a full attendance of village men.

It was at about that time that Trunch combined with five or six neighbouring parishes to promote an annual horticultural show, which was to be held in a different parish each year. A committee was formed of representatives from the villages concerned, and the show took place in late June or early July. In an area filled with dedicated gardeners, its appeal was instantaneous and irresistible. Classes for fruit, flowers and vegetables were divided into two sections – one for cottage gardeners and another for those who employed a gardener. There were several classes for needlework and cookery as well as one for the children's collections of wild flowers. A large marquee added a touch of grandeur to the occasion, and there were few families in the neighbourhood who did not have at least one entrant among the competitors.

Sports Day occupied another Saturday afternoon in the village calendar. It was held on the paddock in front of White

House and run by a committee of men whose wives dished out cups of tea and sticky buns from a table under the central chestnut tree. Mr Spurgeon, the butcher, was armed with a starting-gun, and Mr Humphreys, the people's warden, with a speaking-trumpet. The programme included races of all kinds for all ages and finished up with a men's tug of war between married and single.

The only other sporting activities I remember were connected with the football club. Club matches were played on my grandfather's pasture but, although we children heard a lot about the team's successes or failures, we did not see any matches. One Saturday afternoon I persuaded our maid to go with me. The game was most exciting, and the spectators became very involved in shouting-matches of their own. 'Come yew on! Come yew on!' they yelled, as a Trunch forward shot out of the line, dribbling the ball. 'Dirty Southrepps! Dirty Southrepps!' they bawled, when the opposing team kicked it out of his reach. I became so carried away by all this that I jumped up and down and shouted 'Dirty Southrepps!' with the best of them. There was an instant silence round me, a few giggles from the young, but a great many reproving glances from the older villagers. I was bitterly embarrassed, for I knew that I had done the wrong thing. It was not my place to get over-excited and shout 'Dirty Southrepps!' at a football match.

11. *'Getting About'*

After the war, country roads remained more in keeping with the demands of horse- and foot-traffic than those of the motor car. Signposts were placed high enough to be read at eye-level by the driver of a dog-cart. Road verges were wide, there were triangular pieces of grass where three ways met, and often a green patch at the centre of a crossroads. Clouds of dust blew about in dry weather, and when it rained, the surface of any low-lying road was covered in mud and puddles of water. Occasionally one saw a goat, a donkey or a pony tethered at the roadside, and a farmer who supplied our end of the village with milk frequently sent out his cows to graze the banks.

Two or three local enthusiasts had owned cars since the turn of the century. Our doctor became a motorist some years before the war, and one of my uncles was in possession of a car in 1912. My aunts nicknamed it 'Angelina', and I think it was a Rover. When uncle joined up, he sold her to father, but Angelina became very temperamental, and father soon got rid of her. About 1916, he bought a grey, two-seater Minerva, with a hood, a dickey seat and two hooters – one a bulb horn and the other a klaxon. In comparison with the old-style paraffin lamps, the new acetylene gave a brilliant light. The windscreen was made in two halves: if it rained, hailed or snowed, the upper half could be swung outward to enable the driver to see more clearly, but both he and his passenger had to sacrifice comfort to visibility. The dickey was exposed and could be extremely cold, though not more so than the open pony traps to which we were all well accustomed.

When father gave up his horse, he relied on the car for

'Angelina' – a temperamental car

everyday purposes, leaving the new pony, Jenny, for his wife and children. At Ivy House, my aunts and grandmother used a large pony and cart, but grandfather, who was slowing up, preferred a small pony and trap to get round his farm at a leisurely pace. He owned a succession of old ponies, all of which he called Brownie. One particular Brownie caused a good deal of excitement when it was discovered apparently dead in the stable. The knacker was sent for, but when his sinister little cart appeared on the scene, Brownie was up and pulling at the hay rack.

I do not remember a motorized delivery van in Trunch at that date. Shopkeepers on grocery rounds went out with canvas-covered horse-drawn vans, not unlike the covered waggons pictured in books about the early overseas settlers. The design and condition of other tradesmen's carts varied according to the needs of the owner: they ranged from a smart little turn-out drawn by a lively pony to the flat-bottomed carts drawn by big horses that brought the village coal from the station depot at North Walsham. Some of the old ponies were very reliable. A man who did jobs for my father was a good workman but too fond of the bottle, and if, as occasionally happened, he tumbled out of his cart, the pony always stopped and waited for him to get up again, and if he fell asleep while driving, she brought him home. One day he toppled from the ridge of the barn roof upon the hard road below. He was unhurt, and a passer-by, picking him up, remarked drily that, 'The drink seemed to give him a bounce.'

The small dealers who attended markets and liked to live an independent life possessed horses and carts of one kind or another. Where a lurcher ran underneath the cart, its master was suspected of being a poacher as well as a dealer. Owners of donkeys may have been the survivors of an earlier generation of 'dickey dealers', as they were called. They were usually old men or women who lived in outlying cottages with an acre or two of land where they pastured geese beside the donkey. They did not much use the main roads but frequented back lanes and greenways as they had in their youth. The shaggy little donkeys looked every bit as awkward and independent as their owners.

Among the better-off, bicycles were fairly plentiful, both for pleasure and as a means of transferring oneself from A to B, but there were not many bicycles among the cottage people, and their children were expected to walk to school. If you were able-bodied, walking was not looked upon as a hardship but rather as a natural means of getting about. The network of footpaths and bridleways crossing the fields between various lanes and lokes had been purpose-made by the boots of labouring men, who found it quicker to tramp cross-country to their work than to use the winding and circuitous roads. As long as a path was in use, the stiles were kept up, and where there was a runnel of water, it was bridged by a plank. Water was not drained away so quickly as it now is, and there were little springs here and there about the land, as well as old pit holes and small ponds which filled only during a rainy period. One such pond by the side of the Knapton road was known as the Ha'penny Pit; it was said that many years ago a man lost a halfpenny on the spot and that he dug the hollow in a futile attempt to recover his money.

For a few years after its purchase, father's Minerva was the only car in the village, and in emergencies he helped out by taking the sick or those in need of operations to the hospital at Cromer. He stored a number of tins of petrol in the garage as a reserve fuel supply. The car had a good engine, but roadside punctures were a common occurrence. The hazards of the road were animal rather than mechanical: loose horses, cows pouring out of a field, and horses either ridden or driven who shied away and refused to pass the car.

Before he began growing sugar beet, father kept about a hundred sheep from the end of June until December. They grazed for a time, then finished up behind hurdles, eating turnips. After their arrival, they had to be moved from one field to another at intervals of a day or two. If a motor car appeared behind the flock when it was on the road, it was important that both the sheep and the driver of the car remained calm and that the driver did not sound the horn. In the absence of a dog, an energetic child could be of great assistance in moving sheep, and I especially enjoyed the moment when I beckoned the car to come in behind me while I walked a yard or two in front of it – seeing the white, woolly backs divide to either side (rather like the Red Sea and the Israelites) – until the car got through and its occupants waved a farewell.

An open car gave one a tremendous sensation of speed at twenty-five miles an hour, but in a dry summer speed equated with grit and blinding dust. Mother and the aunts wore special light coats, veils over their faces and wide-brimmed straw hats tied under their chins with pale, gauzy scarves. In winter, a cold snap was the enemy. We wore our thickest clothing and wrapped ourselves round with rugs. If it was freezing cold and we had some distance to go, mother might produce a large stone hot-water bottle for the feet, or even a hot baked potato to keep our hands warm and help to prevent chillblains. Ladies carried fur muffs in winter and sometimes concealed a baked potato in them, but grandmother possessed a Doulton muff-warmer, shaped like a miniature hot-water bottle, which she said was helpful.

One could become very cold and wet when driving behind a pony in an open trap. My aunts had an enormous black umbrella, capable of sheltering four or five people. They also owned an equally large, pale green sunshade for hot-weather driving but did not often use it.

Journeys by car and pony trap took us only where the grown-ups decided to go, and they liked to stick to the main roads. Our childish walks were escorted and did not extend far beyond the parish boundary. When my brother and I were given bicycles, it added a new dimension to our lives. I was about nine years old, and he two years younger. Away on our own, we soon realized how little we knew of the lanes and byroads outside our own parish. We did not go far – at most within a radius of five or six miles – but each ride was an exploration, and our horizons widened as we pedalled along.

The railway was the most popular means of long-distance travel. There were two stations at North Walsham and an excellent service to London as well as to Norwich and Yarmouth. If one wished to venture cross-country, to the Midlands or West of England, and was prepared for innumerable waits and changes of trains, one boarded the 'Old Muddle and Go Nowhere', as the M&GN line was called. When a depression hit agriculture in the 1890s, some of the younger labourers left the land in order to take up more lucrative, though temporary, jobs as navvies, working on local extensions of the railway. 'I was odd-job boy at old Mr Bidwell's,' said the team man on a neighbouring farm. 'I'd been with him three year and still got the same wage – which wor'n't much. One day, I went to him and said: "Marster, when are you going to hain me?" [raise my wages]. He took a look at me and said: "I are'nt!" So I quit the farmwork and went into navvying. When things got better, I come back again.'

The licensee of the New Inn provided our village public transport. As well as his black cab, he kept an old waggonette for hire. I never saw it in use but was told that it would seat six or eight people. Large packages could be sent to Norwich via a carrier's cart which passed through the village twice weekly.

Country roads carried so little traffic that North Walsham appeared to be an extremely busy town, and Norwich was our metropolis. Whenever we drove into the city with father on a Saturday morning, we checked the time it took the car to traverse the length of Magdalen Street. Ten minutes was considered a speedy passage, and twenty minutes or longer was not unusual. The trams were all over the road, and bicycles shot along on either side of the car. When we arrived at the post office crossroads and were beckoned over it by the white-gloved hands of a large policeman who stood at the centre, we were ready to agree that our policemen were simply wonderful – and how did they manage to preserve their Olympian calm in the face of so much traffic?

'Farmers do not go away on holidays,' said father, and, as a family, we did not do so. Very few of the people we knew went on holiday either, so we did not feel we were missing anything. The holiday-makers we encountered during July and August came from London and the South of England. 'Down south, they spend their money as soon as it is in their pockets!' declared a neighbouring farmer.

The southern spendthrifts were usually pleasant couples enjoying an annual holiday in a seaside area where they and their families had access to clean, sandy beaches and unspoiled countryside. To Norfolk farm children, they were about as foreign as if they had come from the other side of the Channel, and we knew without being told that their way of life was not the same as ours. The mothers enjoyed sketching and painting in water-colours. They were often to be seen sitting on a camp stool before an easel set up outside the yard gate, busily recording the picturesque scene of pump, pond, thatched pub and medieval church, while their husbands walked the children round the rest of the village. The artists always gave me a polite 'Good morning' as I passed the easel, and I said 'Good morning' to them in an equally polite manner – but was there a faint note of patronage on the one side and a hint of bucolic aggression on the other?

To some people the very word 'holiday' carried an undertone of slightly decadent frivolity. If you left home, there had to be a reason for it. The parish was accustomed to the idea of young men and women who travelled long distances, either to war or to earn a living. Among my own family, there were two uncles and a great-uncle in Canada, another uncle and great-uncle who had worked in South Africa and a great-uncle who had disappeared while prospecting for gold in Australia. My father had worked in Canada, as well as taking part in the Boer War, and later on two of his younger brothers fought in France. This was in no way remarkable: a similar story could have been told in many farmhouses and cottages. But if the brother or sister of a cottage emigrant was able to save the fare for an overseas visit, it was described not as a holiday but as 'lending a hand with the harvest' or 'keeping an eye on things while Emma has her sixth'.

The intense parochialism that coloured the village outlook was perhaps more an attitude of mind than a matter of mileage, for the fact of having relations abroad did little to widen the horizon or combat prejudices against those 'foreigners' near at hand. In Trunch there were plenty of elderly folk who knew no other town than North Walsham, four miles away, while many of the younger children had never been outside the parish boundary. Yet, when you heard them talk, you would think that the idea of going to Canada or the States, Africa or the Antipodes was more natural to cottage people than a proposal to venture over the county border into Suffolk.

12. *Health and Medicine*

During the First World War, country people were better fed than those in the towns, so afterwards they showed more resistance to disease and escaped the worst of a terrible epidemic of influenza. On the whole, Trunch was a healthy parish. Children suffered the usual run of infectious illnesses – scarlet fever and diphtheria were the ones to be dreaded. Smallpox was on its way out, and the district isolation hospital in the middle of heathland near Cromer was used to nurse scarlet fever cases. Tuberculosis (or 'consumption', as we called it) was less prevalent than in our parents' youth.

There was no magic cure for other infections, and victims spent quite long periods in bed or in a state of convalescence. Pneumonia was frequently a killer, and bronchitis had to be taken seriously. A cut hand or even a pricked finger could become inflamed and lead to blood-poisoning: if the swelling did not respond to domestic bandaging and poultices, the patient usually decided to consult a doctor when, as one of them said, 'I saw the red begin to go up my arm.'

The family doctor was a friend as well as a physician, and when he was also a good Christian, his influence could be as great as that of a priest. He knew a lot about his patients; he had seen many of the younger ones come into the world, and his knowledge of their weakness and strength in the light of family history assisted him in his diagnosis.

Our doctor lived at North Walsham. As a young man, he had taken over the practice from his father, and by the time he reached middle age, he could read his patients almost as easily as the books on local history he enjoyed in his spare time. He was a big man, with a friendly manner that inspired confidence.

The village carpenter made the coffin, and the sexton dug the grave

The North Walsham doctors ran their practices on an independent basis, did their own dispensing and were always on call unless they made special arrangements. Dr Shepheard's surgery was attached to one end of his house; it contained a consulting-room, a dispensary and a small waiting-room with a wooden table in the middle and a wooden bench all round the walls. Panel patients opened the street door into a narrow hallway and passed into the waiting-room on the right. Paying patients rang the bell and waited for a maid to show them into the doctor's dining-room on the left. Wherever they were, when the doctor was free he appeared at a connecting door to call them into his consulting-room. If a box of pills or a bottle of medicine had to be collected, you opened the street door and found your neatly labelled box or bottle on a shelf inside the hall.

From time to time, mother took us to a dentist at North Walsham, but most of the villagers eschewed dental care and relied upon their doctor to pull out a tooth when it gave trouble. Our doctor was renowned for his skill at pulling teeth, and it was said that, 'He would have it out before you knew anything about it!'

Surgical operations took place at either Cromer or Norwich, while a determined effort was being made to raise enough money to build a cottage hospital at North Walsham. The best of the nursing homes contained small operating theatres. Cromer had a nursing home as well as a convalescent home for patients from the Norfolk & Norwich Hospital, and there were a number of nursing homes in Norwich. As long as one could afford it and had the accommodation and domestic help, there was no difficulty about engaging a trained nurse to live in and take charge of a patient at home.

It was generally understood and accepted that a doctor charged his patients according to their means, so that those who paid helped to contribute to the costs of those who could not. But the inhabitants of Trunch were not likely to trouble him unnecessarily; the village had no telephone, and an urgent request for medical attention at home involved journeys either to North Walsham or to the doctor at Mundesley. If one or two parish hypochondriacs demanded an occasional bottle of some harmless mixture (as long as it was pink, with a bitter taste, they were sure it did them good), there were others who refused to ask for help until it was too late. Then, for the most part, the incurables suffered in silent patience and, as with sick cattle, only their eyes revealed a dumb endurance of pain. 'What can't be cured, must be endured' was all they would tell you about it.

Country men and women were realistic but at the same time reverent and caring in the face of death. Sara Ann and a few of the older women were ready to help nurse a serious illness and in the event of death would do whatever was necessary. The sexton dug the grave, while the village carpenter made the coffin and took charge at the funeral. The coffin was taken to church either upon the parish bier or upon the shoulders of the mourners or their friends. It was customary for a farmer to make his last journey upon the shoulders of six of his men, and if members of his family died, they were carried in the same way.

At any funeral, all the relatives of the deceased wore black, and the cottagers were dressed in the deepest possible mourning – not a touch of white anywhere. Occupants of the better-off houses kept special black-edged notepaper and envelopes for correspondence during bereavement and for writing letters of condolence to others. Some people used black-rimmed calling-cards. On the first Sunday after a village funeral, it was usual for the bereaved family to attend Matins: the village pecking-order was set aside and, whatever their social status, on that day the sad little party had an accepted right to sit in a front pew and get what comfort they could from the parson's sermon and the unspoken support of the congregation.

'Cleanliness is next to godliness' was the motto of the majority of housewives, and their efforts were almost on a par with the standards enforced in hospitals and nursing homes. Yet soap and water and disinfectant did not eradicate all the minor bodily upsets: during summer, bilious attacks and sick headaches were common to all ages, but more especially to the young. In warm weather, it was a continuing problem to prevent milk going sour and keep food fresh. A few of the cottages possessed cellars, almost all had good pantries and a fly-proof meat safe in a cool place outside. In the larger houses and farms, there were dairies and storerooms as well as cellars and meat safes. Yet people grumbled that, 'The flies have got at the joint' or that, 'The morning's milk was gone before dinner-time.' When it turned hot and thundery, mother boiled all the milk as soon as it was brought in; milk, as well as butter and some other foods, was kept in the cellar, which was the only place in the house where jellies or blancmanges could be induced to set.

Blue-bottles were the culprits as far as meat was concerned but, from mid-June onwards, house flies were the worst nuisance. They tormented the cattle, and the team man suspended a branch of elder over the head of each of his horses to keep the flies away from their eyes. Indoors, flies buzzed about the window panes and hovered round the food. At Ivy House, my grandmother had two large oil lamps with crimson shades hanging from the ceiling above the dining-table: for some reason, a cloud of house flies circled endlessly below each lamp. Flies liked anything sweet, so the jam dishes, sugar bowls and milk jugs on the tea table were protected by circles of white net, edged with crochet work and a trim of coloured beads. Apart from swatting them, the only method of attack was to hang up fly-papers; the sticky coating trapped masses of the insects, but the long papers were so unsightly, as well as messy when they touched clothing, that their use was restricted to the kitchen. The tiny black 'midges', or corn thrips, that were with us for a few days before harvest, settled upon the windows and walls of a room but did not interfere with food.

Mother was always inclined to be suspicious of food eaten away from home, especially when its source was unknown to her. One of the aunts took me to Norwich for the day and, after showing me the cathedral, decided it would be a good idea to have a walk on Mousehold Heath, a beautiful unspoilt area on the other side of the river. It was a June day and we were beginning to feel hot and thirsty, when we heard the sound of tinkling bells, and down the road came an Italian ice-cream cart, rattling along behind a smart pony. The cart was painted in cheerful colours, with a striped awning above the container. The driver was very foreign-looking, with a black moustache and a broad smile. Perched beside him sat a monkey, clothed in red and green. I could not believe my eyes! I was nine years old, and it was the first time I had eaten an ice, but I do not remember the taste – only the jollity of the Italian ice-cream cart and mother's annoyance when she heard about the incident – 'Whatever can your aunt have been thinking about?' she said. 'Why, you might both have been poisoned!' On another occasion, when we were walking round the market stalls with her on a Saturday, my brother suggested buying a saucer of cockles, but mother told him he would be sure to have typhoid if he ate them.

Fear of sleeping in a damp, unaired bed was a well-founded obsession based upon the dread of contracting rheumatic fever. We were told that rheumatic fever led to heart trouble and other illnesses – the invalids were never the same again. Mother had two very large Doulton bed-warmers which she kept for airing the spare beds. Bedrooms were always cold in winter unless there was a fire in the grate, and even then it was not easy to maintain the accepted sick-room temperature of 60° Fahrenheit. Rheumatism, or 'the screws' as it was called, was common in later life, and there were many suggested but few apparent cures. To carry a potato in the pocket was said to be an easy way to immunize oneself, though it did not work for everyone. Ladies recommended drinking celery tea, and men afflicted with lumbago found that a length of binder twine tied round the waist next to the skin provided relief.

Cottage medication was a mixture of common sense and superstition. A combination of port wine and brandy was known as an infallible cure for diarrhoea, and rural remedies for chillblains, warts, whitlows and styes were legion. Rubbing the affected hands or feet with fresh snow was the best way to get rid of chillblains, but warts were a more difficult problem. You began by rubbing them with one of a variety of unlikely curatives. Old Smith, from Back Street, assured us that a dodman (snail) would give the best results: '... and arter yew ha' rubbed it on,' he said, 'du yew hull that there dodman inter the deeke and don't yew say nothing to nobody!'

Mother gave us nothing but doctor's medicine. She did not believe in old wives' tales. If a medicine tasted nasty (and most of them did), we were told to hold our noses while we drank it. As a child, my eldest aunt had been at the receiving end of a weekly dose of brimstone and treacle; she said it was horrible. Later on, as fashions changed, the accepted purgative became castor oil, and this she took to the end of her life. After she reached the age of ninety, her doctor suggested a change to a milder aperient, but she told him that castor oil had always suited her. Many of the oldest inhabitants had been reared with the help of a tansy pudding in the springtime (to ward off worms) and did not remember it with affection. Patches of tansy, often accompanied by clumps of horse-radish, persisted on old roadside sites from which the cottages had long since disappeared.

Chemists were asked to prescribe for both man and beast. Some of the villagers preferred to consult a chemist about a minor ailment and pay him a few pence for the suggested remedy rather than sit around in a doctor's surgery waiting for cheaper advice and medicine.

The local veterinary surgeons worked with horses, cattle and other farm animals and had little time or inclination to deal with household pets. An experienced old chemist in North Walsham prescribed for dogs, cats and small animals, and his customers had complete faith in his physic. We knew a lady who kept a few hens in her back garden: two years earlier, the oldest bird had been revitalized by a pill from this chemist, and from that day onwards the owner bought pills on a regular basis and the hen appeared at the back door every morning at 8 a.m. to receive her daily pick-me-up.

Our tractor-driver thought he had a stye coming when the corner of his eye began to swell in an alarming manner. He was a man whose deep-set eyes were half concealed by long eyelashes and very bushy eyebrows. After some days, during which the eye became progressively more painful and inflamed, it finally closed up, so he decided to go to the doctor. The doctor thought that his trouble might be an ingrowing eyelash and sent him to hospital. At Norwich, it was discovered that an oat, imbedded among the dense hairs at the corner of his eye and watered by the moisture produced by the irritation it created, had germinated and was doing its best to take root.

The older men smoked pipes, while younger ones preferred a cigarette. The village boys smoked Woodbines, which were the cheapest and good value for money, but the tobacco was loosely packed and the cigarettes dangled from their mouths, the thin, outer paper stained yellow and brown with nicotine. Father's pipe was like a companion to him; he never smoked cigarettes but would get out a box of cigars at Christmas or on special occasions. Mother and her contemporaries said that they had begun smoking during the war, but, while they made no secret of it, they appeared to enjoy their cigarettes in solitude or in the company of one another, rather than when their husbands were around.

A doctor did not discourage his patients from putting on weight. He might himself be of a comfortable size. In 1920, it was no sin to be fat, and teenaged girls were expected to look lumpy and go through an awkward age before their metamorphosis into slim and attractive eighteen- or nineteen-year-olds. It was considered natural for members of both sexes to become stout in later life. 'Eat what you like and what you can afford' was the maxim of country people, who worked very hard physically, slept well and had few digestive troubles.

A woman whose husband was a victim of prolonged stomach trouble acted on the principle of 'A little of what you fancy does you good' when, as a last resort, she treated the poor man to a raw kipper – 'Because,' she explained, 'he's that fond on 'em.' In a roundabout way, the kipper did do him good, for when her final remedy failed, his wife called in the doctor.

13. *The Rhythm of the Year – Household Events*

The ancient cycle of seedtime and harvest was supplemented by a domestic overlay of tradition and custom. The year took on its own rhythm as it followed an annual sequence of household events which were routine to parents but fresh and interesting to their children.

After the excitements of Christmas, the New Year arrived quietly and, though mother and father sat up to see it in, its advent was marked in no other way. As the days went by, mother's thoughts turned to making marmalade. Sweet oranges appeared in the shops during the winter months, but Sevilles were the oranges with which she was most concerned. Every year, she made at least 100 pounds of marmalade, and sometimes double that amount. It was quite a laborious occupation, as all the peel was sliced thinly by hand and the jars covered by circles cut from sheets of greaseproof paper tied on with fine string. During the latter half of January, the kitchen end of the house was full of the spicy smell of boiling fruit. Sometimes the oranges were very dirty and, as she scrubbed them, Maud used to tell us that the Spaniards rolled their oranges along the streets all the way from the orchards to the sea.

14 February was St Valentine's Day and an evening of family excitement for children all over the village. The saint was known to us as 'Old Father Valentine' – as mysterious as Father Christmas, because, though everyone knew about him, no one saw him and he brought presents. But Valentine was a bit of an eccentric, lacking the comfortable benevolence of Father Christmas. His gifts were small – a bar

Turnip lanterns for Guy Fawkes night

of chocolate, perhaps even a single toffee – but they were always well wrapped and labelled with the name of the recipient.

The old lady who had tea with us on Valentine's Day enjoyed the fun as much as mother. After tea we sat about in the dining-room, impatiently wondering when 'He' would come. A thunderous knock upon the back door announced his arrival, but when we rushed to open it, a present lay on the mat and there was no sign of the saint. Sometimes he banged at the back door, sometimes on the front. The parcels were all shapes and sizes, or it might be that there was no parcel at all. When layer after layer of paper was removed from an unexpectedly large package, it was found to contain only a piece of coal. Occasionally, whoever opened the door saw a present slither from the mat and disappear into darkness round the corner. Mother said that the old man liked a joke, and she thought he must keep a reel of black cotton in his pocket. When we were small, it did not occur to us to wonder why mother or Maud should be a bit breathless, but as we grew older and wiser, we liked to pretend we still 'believed' – as much for our own pleasure as for the sake of the younger children.

Spring cleaning started in a quiet way as soon as the days began to lengthen, and continued unobtrusively until mother decided that the chimneys of the principal rooms must be swept – 'before', as father used to say, 'the women really turn the house upside down'. Sweeping chimneys was a dirty business, both for the sweep and for the housewife. The rooms containing the chimneys to be swept were prepared on the previous day: everything small was put out of the way, the furniture was veiled in dustsheets, and the floors were covered in all directions with old newspapers. At five o'clock the following morning, the sweep arrived on a bicycle. His brushes were strapped to the framework and stuck out some way behind him. As he had cycled four or five miles from North Walsham, he was given tea and bread and butter before starting work. From then on, the house echoed to strange sounds and muffled bumps as his brushes explored the cavernous insides of the old chimneys. By nine o'clock, all was finished; a thin film of soot was visible on the dustsheets and considerably more on the mantelpieces and round the hearths. The interior of the house had a faintly acrid smell. 'You need a man who understands old chimneys like I do, Ma'am,' said the sweep, now black in the face and with the whites of his eyes showing in an unusual manner. He washed his hands at the sink before consuming another pot of tea and a plate of sandwiches, accepted his money and rode away out of our sight until the same time next year. He left the soot behind him, and it was used to help manure the garden or keep the slugs at bay.

A great deal of yellow soap was used in the course of spring cleaning, but often furniture polish and scouring-powder were made at home. There was not much choice of such things in the shops. If you wanted to bring up the colour of a carpet as well as to clean it, a good sprinkling of used tea-leaves applied before the final brushing or vacuum cleaning was said to produce excellent results.

A friend of mother's who liked to try something new was told by a butcher's wife that the best way to rejuvenate a carpet was to wash it with liquid in which the gall bladder of an ox had been steeped for several days. 'Indeed,' said the friend, 'the butcher's wife did have a very pretty carpet; but after she showed me an ox gall, I decided to stick to my tea-leaves!'

Lent was heralded by pancakes on Shrove Tuesday. I do not remember eating them at any other time of the year. It was correct to serve pancakes with lemon and sugar, but jam was permissible for children. During Lent, we had fish on Fridays, and my aunts seemed to go to church more frequently than usual. On Good Friday, the hot cross buns were large and spicy and sticky, and the baker made his delivery at six o'clock in the morning because his customers liked to eat them at breakfast. On Easter Sunday, everyone went to church. If we had new clothes, we wore them for the first time, and at dinner we ate the traditional baked custard after our roast beef.

When eggs became plentiful, a large earthenware pot in the cellar was cleaned out and filled with a fresh solution of waterglass – all ready to put down the surplus eggs as soon as they were brought indoors. Eggs would keep for a year in waterglass; they were not very nice boiled, fried or poached but could be used for baking at times when the hens were in moult or when cold weather caused them to go off the lay.

We played with tops and hoops like other children, but two of our favourite games in the early part of the year were dependent upon a clump of bamboo in the shrubbery and a group of elder bushes near the cart shed. Bamboo was invaluable when an urge of spring filled us with the desire to make bows and arrows. A Christmas gift of a new penknife came in handy as we chose a strong but flexible cane for the bow and shorter, thinner pieces for the arrows. String from the kitchen drawer and a bit of elder wood to tip the arrows completed our armament.

One could fashion a whistle from elder by removing the pith from a piece of last year's wood and making the appropriate cuts, but we used it in a more interesting way when we built ourselves little dens at the time of year when the elders came into leaf. One of the farm men showed us how to cut lengths of the straight growths which followed an annual hedge-cutting, and tie them criss-cross with string until we had four panels of similar size. Three of the panels were pegged into the ground, while a fourth was placed upon the top and more string or binder twine used to hold the erection together. Then branches of elder in full leaf were tucked into the framework, until the whole thing resembled a leafy little hut with an open front. In later life, it is tempting to visualize a connection between the pattern of those juvenile hide-outs and the earlier shelters built by little boys who had to spend long, lonely days scaring crows – or even to think of them as humble descendants of the summer bowers said to have been so beloved by Saxon and early medieval ladies.

April was the month when gypsy women called at the back door. There were usually two of them, either selling clothes pegs made from split hazel wood or peddling lace. With their black hair, brown faces, dark eyes and quick, lively speech, they were quite unlike any of the people we knew. Year after year, the family camped for a short time at the entrance of a green lane just outside the village. A young woman could be seen stirring the pot above a smoking wood fire, while two or three brown little children played around her, apparently indifferent to either rain or sunshine.

Whit Sunday was the traditional day on which to eat the first gooseberry pie, but there were years when Whitsun came too early for gooseberries, and cooks had to make do with a jar of bottled fruit from the store cupboard. The squirrel's instinct was highly developed in countrywomen, and even those with large gardens saw to it that all the fruit was picked or picked up, jammed, bottled, given away or stored. Mother made more jam than marmalade and had been known to dispatch Maud to turn out some of our caterpillars if she ran short of jars. She bottled gooseberries and raspberries as well as a great many plums. The plum crop was notoriously erratic; there were years when branches broke under the weight of the fruit, and others when the yield was little or nothing.

Father stored his apples and pears in a disused room of the house, but grandfather's crop was kept in a detached building which had been methodically fitted out with racks and bins and neat labels for the different varieties. To be taken into the apple house by an aunt to select a basketful of her special red apples for Christmas was quite a ceremonial experience. The place seemed so quiet and remote as we breathed the apple-scented air and listened to her stories about the different trees, their ages and the people who had planted or grafted them. At that time of year, there was always a marrow on the window sill. Most people kept one or two of their largest marrows in a dry place until November or December. When the fruit was yellow and fully ripe, it was used to make pies and open tarts, marrow-and-ginger jam or chutney. The open tarts were nicer than the pies: the cooked marrow was mashed up with eggs and cream, sugar, a few currants and some nutmeg.

Families who bought big joints were accustomed to eating a good deal of cold meat, while those who could not afford so much meat consumed large quantities of cheese. They all liked to accompany such meals with a home-made pickle, preferably one which had a bit of a bite to it. Pickled onions and yellow mixed pickles were the village favourites, and mother also pickled red cabbage and made apple chutney from windfalls.

As long as father kept pigs, we had one 'killed into the house' about once a year – usually in autumn, as soon as the weather became colder. When the animal's diet had included a quantity of milk, the pork was exceptionally tender and well flavoured. The butcher took away the pig selected for slaughter, returning a day or two later with the carcase cut into joints, the bladder and intestines cleaned and the 'fry' and meat for sausages in neat parcels. There was always a large parcel of bones. When everything was disposed on and around the long wooden table in the back kitchen, children were shooed outside and mother and Maud set to work.

After all the fat had been cut into small pieces and was sizzling quietly on the range, mother minced and seasoned the meat set aside for sausages; and when she used her machine to feed the mixture into the prepared intestines, the sausages emerged as a long tube which she pinched and twisted to form the conventional shapes. There was no bread or biscuit meal in home-made sausages. The pig's internal fat made the best lard, so it was rendered down separately and stored either in jars or in the bladder. The small, crisp remnants left in the pan could be used to make a 'scrap pie'. This was a spicy patty, baked on a plate, with a filling of scraps mixed with a few currants, sugar, lemon peel and nutmeg.

The best of the smaller, meaty bones was used to make 'bone pies' which were eaten cold and had a thick pastry crust, the bones and meat embedded in a delicious jelly below. The remaining bones were simmered slowly in a large boiler for several hours. As they cooled, the stock was strained off and the shreds of meat were separated from the bones. After removing the fat, the stock was again simmered to reduce it to the desired consistency before adding the meat, seasoning and, possibly, a few sliced hard-boiled eggs. Finally the brownish liquid full of little pieces of meat was ladled into moulds and basins. This was the way to make a true Norfolk pork cheese. It set to a light but firm jelly.

The various cuts of bacon and the hams, all of which had been previously rubbed with salt, were drained and placed in large earthenware crocks where the prepared brine or pickle was poured over them. The joints were turned and the liquid spooned over them daily for three or four weeks; but if a woman was menstruating, she was not allowed to go near the pork, for if she so much as touched it with a spoon, the meat was sure to go bad. Everyone believed this, and many said that they had had personal experience of its occurrence.

The process of dealing with the parts of the pig was spread over several days. Many of the sausages and pork cheeses were made to be given away, for without refrigeration their edible life was a short one, but the bacon and hams were sent to North Walsham to be smoked, and afterwards they were enclosed in coarse linen bags and hung in one of the attic rooms. A joint of bacon was kept in the dairy, and whenever bacon was wanted, the slices were cut from it by hand.

With the coming of November, children's thoughts revolved round the chance of getting hold of a good-sized turnip – the larger the better – to make a turnip lantern for Guy Fawkes Day. It took a long time to chip out the interior of the root, and a little help from older members of the family was welcomed, but the child finished it off by cutting two round eyes and a wide, grinning mouth through the face of the hollowed shell. Then all that was needed was a piece of string for a handle and a candle to fix inside before one became the proud owner of a turnip lantern. When you watched two or three of these illuminated turnip faces swinging into the yard on a dark evening, you might well have been scared had you not heard the giggles of the children who carried them.

On the evening of the 5th, the greater part of the village was too occupied to be interested in bonfires, and I do not remember ever hearing anything about fireworks. It was the night when village children dressed themselves in whatever weird and wonderful garments they or their mothers could devise, before walking out to visit some of their relations and do a round of the bigger houses in quest of 'a penny for the poor old guy'. Little groups of children were arrayed in clothes ranging from a piratical rig-out to an ancient nightdress that trailed in the mud behind its small wearer. Most of them wore large straw or felt hats acquired at the village jumble sale, and paper masks which were sold at the village shop. As they disguised their voices, it was difficult to identify anyone. Very often, the youngest child would be dressed as a guy and brought along in a pushchair. The guys began to arrive as soon as it was dark, and their visits continued off and on for about two hours.

Each party knocked at the back door and was asked into the kitchen. We admired their costumes and their lanterns and tried in various ways to find out who the children were. They giggled uncontrollably. Then the leader, speaking in a gruff, well-rehearsed voice, asked if we could spare a penny for the poor old guy. 'First, you must dance or give us a song!' demanded Maud, who enjoyed these evenings as much as we did. 'What can you do?' And eventually the visitors would be persuaded to sing or perform a series of hops and skips, which, because of their garments, seemed to be all they could manage in the way of a dance.

We handed round some sweets, mother gave the oldest child a few coppers from the pile she had ready on the kitchen dresser, and our Guy Fawkes guys shuffled off, still giggling and probably still unknown to us, the light from their turnip lanterns weaving an uncertain path towards the yard gate.

After Guy Fawkes, the domestic talk was all about puddings, cakes, turkeys and trees. Our Christmas was traditional and celebrated in much the same way as Christmas is today. We helped or hindered the long task of stoning the raisins and attempted to stir the pudding mixture. But the secular burden of Christmas was firmly on the backs of the grown-ups. Children were cast as the recipients.

14. *Old Rhymes, Sayings and Superstitions*

Looking back, I think that behind the traditional Norfolk façade of thick heads and weather-beaten cheeks there lurked a mishmash of half-understood sayings and visual images handed down to them through their forebears. The villagers were not articulate enough to rationalize inherited fears by

A lucky primrose

At midnight on Hallowe'en

discussing them. Instead, they threw out dark hints which usually related to the doom-and-gloom side of many country legends and superstitions.

Old rhymes and sayings, especially those associated with the weather, were to be heard in everyday conversation; today, many of them are not so well known. Where the origin was of historical or biblical interest, the people were apt to know their Bibles better than they did their history books: 'My grandfather taught me this here,' said the owner of a small farm. 'His father taught it to him, and it is about suffin' what happened a werry long time ago.' His version of the two-edged, prophetic rumour current in the county before the rising of 1549, that

The country gnoffes, Hob, Dick and Hick
With clubs and clouted shoon
Shall fill the vale of Dussin's Dale
With slaughtered bodies soon

was reasonably exact, and though, like him, I had not then heard of Kett's Rebellion, I sensed a little of the awe and mystery which hung over an unknown Norfolk past.

On the other hand, there was no particular mystery in connection with Nebuchadnezzar. One could read about him in the Old Testament, provided one was able to find the right place. But the Bible gave us no information about a piece of nursery doggerel:

Nebuchadnezzar, the King of the Jews,
Sold his wife for a pair of shoes.
When the shoes began to wear,
Nebuchadnezzar began to swear.

It is said that many of the great events of the past have been whittled down to the status of nursery rhymes or games played by young children. Maybe we were commemorating a little bit of history when we built an extra large sandcastle and one of us stood upon the top of it, shouting defiantly at all and sundry:

I am the King of the Castle
You're a dirty rascal!

Our parents and grandparents told us that, as children, they had played the same game, using any little hillock about the farm in place of a sandcastle on the beach.

Although we knew nothing of the Good King Arthur who once ruled this land and whose Queen had made him such an extremely large plum pudding, the practicalities of the rhyme appealed to the mind of a child.

When Good King Arthur ruled this land
He was a goodly king

He bought three pecks of barley meal
To make a bag pudding.

A bag pudding the Queen did make
And stuffed it well with plums
And in it put great lumps of fat
As big as my two thumbs.

The King and Queen did eat thereof
And noblemen beside
And what they could not eat that night
The Queen next morning fried.

The Queen, like our mother, was evidently thrifty with left-overs.

When an irate mother shouted at a child: 'If you do that again, boy, I'll skin you alive!' the words meant no more to either of them than the threat of a smart slap on the bottom, but the phrase may have revealed the lingering folk memory of an unspeakable horror. The village girls were quick to call 'Tell-tale tit!' if one of them betrayed a confidence. Occasionally they let fly with the whole verse:

Tell-tale tit!
Your tongue shall be slit!
And all the dogs in the town
Shall have a little bit!

Yet they had never heard of the Seven Deadly Sins, knew nothing of the Roman Catholic Church and certainly had not the faintest idea that the old rhyme referred to a medieval punishment for the Sin of Gossip.

A number of songs and sayings were associated with particular days, such as Shrove Tuesday, certain of the Saints' Days and 5 November. Other jingles were seasonal or brought in the names of local villages. When children made their annual visits on Guy Fawkes Night, their usual chant of 'Remember, remember, the fifth of November' was varied by a more bloodthirsty little song:

Guy Fawkes Guy,
Hit him in the eye!
Hang him on a lamp post
And there let him die!

The first three days of March were expected to usher in the winds needed to dry out the land and ensure the preparation of a good seed bed:

First come David
Then come Chad
Then come Winnold
Roaring mad!

If the wind was in the east on 21 March, it was likely to continue in that quarter until Midsummer.

The weather-wise kept a close eye on the oak and the ash to see if the order of the emerging leaves heralded a dry or a wet summer, while on warm spring days parental repetitions of 'Ne'er cast a clout till May be out!' were guaranteed to drive sweating children to rebellion and the surreptitious removal of their winter-weight Chilprufe combinations.

Two rhymes had been handed down in my father's family from the time of his great-grandmother. The first, believed to have had its origin in relation to crow-scaring, was turned, at a later date, into an action song that never failed to amuse a small child.

Clap two hands [clap hands]
Ring two bells [touch ears]
Knock at the door [touch nose]
And cry Carr Hoo! [lift hands above head and shout]

The old lady's second rhyme could be made intensely dramatic and was often recited to divert a child's attention during the unpopular process of cutting toe-nails or finger-nails:

This little toe was small boy Sam
Went to the cupboard after some jam.
This little toe said: 'Oh, No! No!'
This little toe rather wanted to go.
This little toe said: 'Tisn't quite right',
And this little toe curled quite out of sight.
Down came the jar with a big Slam! Slam!
And this little toe got all the jam.

The moon was a fertile source of rural superstition. Mother had a horror of seeing the new moon through glass, and though father said it was only a silly game, he turned over the money in his pocket and bowed to the yellow crescent before going indoors. To see the old moon with the new was a sign of stormy weather, and the old adage

Saturday new and Sunday full
Never good and never wull

was looked upon as infallible.

If the light of a full moon was allowed to fall upon one's face during sleep, it could 'turn one's brain'. It was an established fact (we were told) that those even slightly deranged became much worse at the time of a full moon. The friendly, familiar stars faded away when the moon was at the full, the garden and fields were irradiated by a cold, eerie light, bright enough to read by, and owls hooted incessantly. It was as if the stage was set for an emergence of superstitious fears.

These were the nights when the great black ghost dog, 'Old Shuck', was most likely to walk the lanes leading to the coast; some said he was headless – but, with or without a head, if his red eyes glowered at you, you knew you would die within a year. The fear of Old Shuck was quite real, and it certainly helped to keep the roads empty at night. Coaches drawn by headless horses or driven by headless coachmen were said to be common enough, but they did not pass through Trunch and were more likely to emerge from isolated churchyards in neighbouring villages.

At night, the yellow glow of an oil lamp or the flicker of

candles was without menace but incapable of illuminating the darker corners of a farmhouse. Long passages were alarming to children at night, while candles and hand-lamps created their own mysterious shadows. It seemed natural enough for us to share a half-hearted belief in ghosts with the rest of the village. If the supernatural was not often mentioned, it was because of an ingrained fear that speech might bring it to life. If one pried too deeply and asked too many questions, one was told 'not to talk it up', and the subject would be changed.

The minds of some of the villagers (especially the women) were constantly occupied by the necessity of a superstitious avoidance of bad luck and the encouragement of good. Many of the ladies declared that, although they did not believe in these practices, they thought it best to be on the safe side. Their lives moved to a complicated rhythm as they threw salt over their left shoulders but refused to look at the new moon from a similar angle. They might decline to undertake a particular task on a certain day of the week. Some women were terrified of thunder; they shut themselves up in cupboards or hid under the stairs until the worst of a storm was over. Others were assiduous readers of tea-cups, could tell one's fortune from the dregs and spot any tall or short stranger who might be contemplating a visit.

It was considered dreadfully unlucky to bring either May blossom or yew into the house, and poppies were taboo. One must not kill a robin, and whatever you were doing when you first heard the cuckoo was sure to become your chief occupation during the year. Although it was not right to do unnecessary work on Good Friday, if bread was baked on that day it would never go mouldy and was said to be a splendid cure for diarrhoea. It was unlucky to cut your nails on a Sunday, and the following rhyme emphasized the days on which to do the job:

> Cut them on Monday, cut them for health.
> Cut them on Tuesday, cut them for wealth.
> Cut them on Wednesday, cut them for news.
> Cut them on Thursday, a new pair of shoes.
> Cut them on Friday, cut them for sorrow.
> Cut them on Saturday – see your sweetheart tomorrow.

A baby's nails should not be cut until the child was a year old but, if necessary, the mother could bite the nails to shorten them.

If a girl found a four-petalled primrose and placed it in her shoe, the first man she met was likely to become her husband; or, if she managed to remain awake long enough to look into her mirror at midnight on Hallowe'en, she would see the shadowy face of her future husband peering over her shoulder. Another rhyme passed down from father's great-granny might have been entitled 'The Right Time for a Girl to Get Married'. Beginning with the age of seventeen, when 'She can pick and she can choose', it ended with the lines:

> But when a girl is thirty-three
> She can sit on a fence, hollerin 'Who'll have me?'

One November day, a woman brought to my mother the root of a perennial she called a snake plant. 'As long as you have it in your garden, Ma'am,' she said solemnly, 'you'll never be bitten by a snake. I shall feel more comfortable about you, Ma'am, if I know you have a piece of my snake plant. Since I had it give me, I've always been so pleased that I needn't be afraid of snakes no more.' When spring arrived, the snake plant was slow to surface, and mother feared she had lost it. Then a shoot was seen, and such rapid growth followed that the plant needed a stake. Eventually an arum-like head appeared, which was the nearest thing to a snake that had ever been seen in our garden.

Birds were believed to mate on St Valentine's Day, and after Michaelmas it was not wise to go blackberrying because on that day the Devil laid his hand on the fruit. At midnight on Christmas Eve the cattle were said to turn towards the east and go down on one knee to salute the Christ Child. Thistles should never be cut before Midsummer, and rain on St Swithin's Day brought forty wet days to follow. Stones in the fields were known to grow. Then there were whispers of ghostly visitants seen in lonely churchyards, and if you were brave enough to stand in the church porch at midnight on St

Mark's Eve, you would see the faces of those in the village who were fated to die within the coming year.

Church porches may have been a refuge for the occasional tramp, but they were an habitual resting-place for a woman who spent the greater part of her life wandering about in our corner of east Norfolk. Lou Pestell was said to have been crossed in love when she was a girl. Afterwards she lost her wits and took to the lanes and fields. She was completely harmless but very shy and afraid of people, though quite at ease with animals and birds. She found her sustenance in the hedgerows and the food that kind-hearted folk left in her way when they heard she was in the vicinity. Clothes were put out in the same manner. All she was ever known to ask for was a little hot water to make a cup of tea. A farmer in the area made a hut available to her as a refuge from bad weather and cold nights, but she could not be persuaded to enter it, though in later life she was said to make occasional use of a hayloft or barn containing straw. Above all else, she needed to be outside, and her usual concession to shelter was to sleep in the nearest church porch.

Sara Ann told us this sad history and said that the wanderer was very clean: 'My boy Tom see her a-washing of herself in the stream that run across the footpath field, but when she see him, she shruck out and run away!'

One morning I met Lou Pestell on the road outside our house. She was a short, squat woman – perhaps about forty years old, with blank blue eyes and a smooth skin marred by a lot of brown spots, like dark freckles. She gave me a wild stare as she passed, but I do not think she really saw me. The village people were half afraid of her, though, as they said, 'She never did no harm to nobody.' I think they felt that she was a kind of human link existing halfway between themselves and their superstitious fears. Lou Pestell lived in this way for many years until, finally, she became old and feeble. The local authorities, who had been merciful enough to leave her alone for so long, decided she must be taken into care. No doubt they were kind and it was all for the best, but old Lou could not live under a roof, so she died.

15. *The Remembered Past*

For a few years after the '14–'18 war, farming was relatively prosperous, although grandfather gave warning that, according to his experience as well as his knowledge of the past, such an aftermath was invariably followed by a depression. He told his sons that there might soon come a time to apply the old saying 'Up horn and down corn', if low prices for grain necessitated a change of farming policy. He said that in the old days 'horn' did not refer to cattle, but to sheep. The greater part of his early life had been spent on a small farm belonging to a widowed grandmother, and he could produce such pithy little sayings handed down from the time of the Napoleonic Wars or earlier. His older children were able to remember their great-granny, and three generations had been brought up to regard the old lady as the family oracle. Through her, one might have said we were still in verbal touch with the eighteenth century.

She was the daughter of one small farmer and married to another, and the whole of her life had been lived close to the land. She was bred to realism and stringent economy. Grandfather said she had told him: 'One boy working on a farm is a good boy, two boys is only half a boy and three boys is no boy at all!' She was inclined to be mean with the eggs: 'When the price is high, there are not many to sell,' she used to declare, 'and when they are cheap, it takes such a lot to bring in a shilling.' In her time, the inhabitants of Trunch were not always honest and law-abiding: many of our great-great-grandmother's anecdotes were about smugglers – of how farmer and fisherman between them had hidden the contraband on remote farms and in holes in the ground; it was reckoned that a bit of smuggling assisted a small farmer

Gathering acorns

to settle his sons in larger properties.

When old age caught up with her, in 1881, she lay in bed for many weeks and was not expected ever again to get out of it. But she was a strong-willed woman. At the end of harvest, the family went off to the field to see the last load on its way home, leaving the eldest child, my aunt, then a girl of nine, as company for the old lady. No sooner were they out of the house than the child was ordered to find great-granny's clothes and give her her stick, because she had a mind to dress and go downstairs to see the last load in. The end of harvest was the peak of the farming year, and she must have known that she would never see another.

Somehow, the pair arrived at the foot of the stairs, a chair was placed in the open doorway and when the horses turned in at the yard gate, great-granny was seated, leaning forward on her stick, with the little girl standing beside her. My aunt used to describe the blue-painted waggon piled high with sheaves, the men sitting on top of the load. She said that the horses were decorated with bunches of corn, and there seemed to be such a lot of children – all of them singing and shouting. Her great-granny watched the little procession pass the house and wind its way towards the stackyard. As soon as it was out of sight, she collapsed; the family had difficulty in getting her back to bed, and before long she died.

It was through our great-great-granny that we knew that the village stocks were once in position outside the churchyard gate and that the village pound had been near a farm on the Mundesley road. A pound was a walled enclosure, built of cobble or brick, with a secure entrance. Any animals found straying after dark were liable to be locked up inside it and released to their owners only on payment of a fine. It had no roof, because the walls were too high for a horse or a cow to escape. A local legend, current in both Trunch and Gimingham (where a pound is still standing), told how a simple soul, on finding an owl in the road, thought it should be in the same place as an already imprisoned donkey. But in the morning, to his astonishment the bird had flown.

Grandfather could remember the days when it was usual to

fallow a strip of land on the perimeter of each cornfield. This flowery pathway was of sufficient width for walking or riding, and in a large field some of the older farmers liked to leave enough room for the passage of a pony and trap. If the grass grew too long, it was scythed. And before harvest it was a hospitable country custom for a farmer to invite his friends to Sunday tea and what must have been a very pleasant walk round the crops.

Local farmers had their boots made for them at North Walsham, where the town shoemaker kept lasts for each of his customers and they could choose from several different grades of leather. The village cobbler made boots as well as mending them, but he was said to be not very good at the job.

Grandfather did not care for the twentieth-century innovation of serving a turkey for Christmas dinner. 'You can't beat a good joint of beef,' he used to declare. 'Roast beef was always good enough for my old granny!' To the end of his life, roast beef as well as a turkey was on the table at Ivy House on Christmas Day. Grandfather carved the beef but expected one of his brothers to deal with the turkey. He liked his breakfast sausages or bacon grilled in front of the bars of the kitchen range, and baked apples cooked in the same way. He preferred potatoes boiled in their skins, but the skins had to be removed before the potatoes were brought to the table.

My parents were born in the late 1870s, and they told us that in the eighties village morale was at a low ebb and lacked any restraining influences. An aged rector was at the end of an incumbency of more than fifty years, the old squire (as the village called mother's grandfather) was dead and his family ineffective. Strong beer was cheap, and the only recreation open to most of the village men was to get themselves blind drunk on Saturday night before they staggered home to beat up their wives. Men from Knapton and Gimingham (where there were no public houses) walked to Trunch for their beer, and after closing time the Hill was liable to become an inter-parochial battlefield.

When a new rector and his family appeared on the scene, the situation began to change. Mother said he was a large, unassuming young man but with considerable strength of character. He suited the parish. Under his influence, the affairs of the church slowly returned to normal, a Men's Club was established in addition to a Sunday School, drinking and swearing were cut down, and fighting on the Hill became a thing of the past. The foundations of village life as we knew it in 1920 had been laid.

During my father's youth, Trunch Club, a parish Friendly Society, held its annual dinner in June: it was a big day in the village because the Club Feast, as it was called, was supplemented by a visiting fair and a programme of sports. Father told us that when he was young there was no easy way for a child to earn a few pence, but he and one of his brothers were determined to get some money to spend at the fairground, and they were given a job singling turnips in a field called Great Ladies' Meadow. At that time, the farm men used hoes to give a first chop to the young turnips, but women followed afterwards to single them. It was hand work, and the rows were long and seemed to go on for ever. The little boys' backs ached unceasingly, but they were to be paid a farthing a row and they stuck at it until they had each earned 3d to spend at the fair.

An aunt remembered how, in autumn, children used to go out gathering acorns, either to feed the family pig or, if they could pick up enough to fill a half bushel, to sell to a farmer for a small sum. My eldest aunt was familiar with a bushel measure at an early age, for her mother kept one in the kitchen and on occasion dumped the toddler into it when the child became too much inclined to meddle. A bushel – holding eight gallons – could be a rather smart piece of barn equipment. It was a deep, circular wooden container, often highly varnished and brass-bound, with a brass handle on each side. When corn was measured and sold by volume, father said it was an art to fill a bushel: the contents had to be levelled off and then shaken down enough to ensure that the farmer did not give short weight, but not so much that he was giving away any grain.

My aunts had vague recollections of hearing about harvest suppers held in the tithe barn near the rectory. After the meal, a fiddler played for dancing. The fattest woman in the village was so large – 'as big as Bale oak' – that it took two men to get their arms round her waist, but she was the best dancer in the village and as light as a feather.

Later on, such great national events as Queen Victoria's Jubilee and the coronations of Edward VII and George V were celebrated in the paddock in front of White House. All the inhabitants of the parish were seated at long tables and enjoyed a traditional meal of roast beef and plum pudding. The beef was cooked in the ovens of the larger houses, and the puddings boiled for hours in coppers which had been well scrubbed to purge them of their usual wash-day aroma. The puddings were large ones, cooked in strong, greased linen clothes, not basins. Grandmother said it was astonishing how many could be boiled at one time in a wash-house copper. Plum puddings were a special treat to her family of ten children. Birthday cakes were unknown to them but, instead, a birthday pudding appeared on the dinner table.

Some fascinating books were to be found at Ivy House. Old volumes of *The Spectator* and a leather-bound book of sermons had once belonged to great-great-granny. *Enquire Within*, a reference book of 1864, contained a glorious mixture of household hints, recipes and general information. One might open it to find recipes for pickles, making shoe polish and 'How to Preserve a Bottle of Milk for Eighteen Months', surrounding a column of advice to young ladies, which began:

> If you have blue eyes, you need not languish,
> If you have black eyes, you need not stare.

The mid-nineteenth-century educational books were all of the question-and-answer type, and so was another tattered volume, much loved by the family, who still referred to it for information. Its title was *A Child's Guide to Knowledge*, but they called it *The Book of Know*.

A little rhyme handed down from my great-great-grandmother seems to me to epitomize a world that has vanished from the village scene:

The cock doth crow
To let you know
If you be wise
'Tis time to rise.

It was as the smell of dawn crept into the air, though the night still hung about, that the village cocks began to crow. Their strident cries echoed from farm to farm and from house to house wherever poultry was kept. Harsh and demanding, but at the same time hopeful, it was like the call of the land, and whenever you heard that call, you knew you had to get up and get on with it.

The 'strong man' of the mill

16. *Economy, Honesty, Hard Work and Education*

'Waste not, want not!' was a way of life in 1920. The recent war had nothing to do with it: our parents had been brought up more stringently than we were, and our grandparents regarded the domestic habits of anyone younger than themselves as wasteful.

Country living was well suited to the practice of never throwing anything away if there was the slightest chance that it might one day be of use. Old farmhouses, with rambling attics and cellars as well as a variety of cupboards built into chimney-breasts and thick walls, provided every opportunity for storage, and if the cottages were small, it was astonishing how much their occupants could pack away in an outside shed.

Part of the system was designed to utilize every piece of clothing and household linen in one form or another as long as the threads hung together. The permutations were endless: clothes bought for Sunday best were relegated to everyday use, and when an adult's garments became too shabby, they could be cut down and transformed into something smaller – children's wear or a new blouse from the skirt of an old summer dress. Grandmother said that, when she was young, this was the stage at which women 'turned' their heavier garments and literally re-made them inside out. Older children's clothes were handed down or given away, and the gloves which everyone wore as a matter of course with outdoor coats finished up by protecting hands engaged in gardening or household tasks. Old washleather gloves were both light and flexible and much in demand for domestic use.

As each item of clothing reached its end, the best and brightest of the material was reserved for the next rag or 'piece' rug.

A nice rag rug on the floor in front of the fire in a farm or cottage kitchen provided a long-lasting and cheerful end for many discarded garments. Cutting the remnants into four-inch strips occupied nearly as much time as making a rug. The worker aimed at having enough strips of the same colour to create a wide, dark border and a brightly coloured diamond shape or a roundel as the centrepiece. Pairs of old trousers or a winter coat were suitable for the first, and red was a popular colour for the second, while the remainder of the rug was usually a hotchpotch of whatever might be available. Should one wish to take up rug-making, the only preliminary expense was the purchase of a rug hook designed to grip each 'piece' as it was pulled through a couple of strands in a row of the sacking base. Sacks were an unofficial 'perk' from the farmer's barn and, when it could be obtained, a thinner sack was used to line the back of the finished rug.

The large white damask tablecloths in general use needed careful darning, towels were taped along a torn edge as long as the centre remained sound, and sheets were turned sides to middle. At a later stage, parts of worn-out sheets, pillowcases and any other remnants suitable for making ovencloths or floorcloths, tea towels or dusters were cut to size and machined round the edges. Two deep drawers in our massive kitchen dresser were full of neatly hemmed cloths, dedicated to every facet of household use. As they too reached their end, each one disappeared into a ragbag which was the source of supply for use in the yard and workshop as well as the house.

In 1920, the wool, cotton or flax from which clothes and linen were manufactured lent itself to adaptation for other purposes but was liable to more wear and tear than today's man-made materials. Mother spent hours and hours darning socks and mending clothes, but her darning basket was never empty. She knitted and crocheted as well as making some of the children's clothes, but patchwork must have been outmoded, for the only piece I can remember is an ancient bedspread which was used as a dustsheet when the sweep made his annual visit.

Outdated newspapers had uses other than laying a fire. Their pages lined shelves and cupboards all over the house, although mother thought that pieces of left-over wallpaper looked prettier in the bedroom chests. A previous owner had carefully pasted newspaper all over the interior of the drawers in the kitchen dresser, and the news of 1878 was there to be read by anyone who took the trouble to look for it.

The cheap and convenient parcel post was a stimulus to save brown paper and string. In our house, the larger sheets of wrapping-paper were kept in an attic beside a pile of empty cardboard dress boxes, while string was deposited rather untidily in one of the kitchen drawers. But at Ivy House a cupboard in the long passage was reserved for the storage of newspapers, brown paper, boxes and string; the newspapers were stacked in an orderly fashion, wrapping-paper was folded tidily, and whenever a parcel arrived at the house, the string was unknotted, twisted up neatly and stored in a basket reserved for the purpose. In either house, the purchase of brown paper or string was considered to be an unnecessary extravagance.

When she was a girl, my eldest aunt crocheted a grey, sausage-shaped receptacle for pipelighters. It hung at the side of the fireplace beside grandfather's chair. Later she became a schoolmistress, but whenever she was at home she made a further supply of spills from folded strips of newspaper, and as long as there was a fire in the grate, grandfather used them instead of matches to light his pipe. 'Matches cost money,' he said.

My grandparents adhered to the old custom of beginning fires on 1 October and ending them on 30 April. On 1 May, irrespective of weather, the grates were cleaned out and lined with brown paper, and for the next five months the only fire to be found in the whole of the big old house was the one in the kitchen range. Mother was less of a Spartan and saw no reason why she should not have a fire to sit by when summer evenings grew chilly. Everyone made the greatest possible use of the daylight hours, partly from motives of economy and partly because lamp- or candle-light was not so strong. One was expected to move to a window with needlework or book to catch the last of the daylight before the lamps were brought in.

The pattern of patch and re-make was repeated as far as possible in everything connected with the house or yard. Kettles and saucepans and pails were patched, either with handy little discs sold for the purpose by every ironmonger or else with larger pieces of tin from the farm workshop. Even cinders were sifted and the unburnable residue used to make up the garden paths. A pile of wood in the cart shed and a conglomeration of old iron in a corner of the farmyard were there because one day some of it might be needed for repairs. Domestic or garden implements were worn down to the limit of use before being discarded, and over the years their owners became attached to the most mundane tools. One of my aunts, an excellent cook, had a favourite wooden spoon with which she beat up the family cakes and puddings. After a long time, she wore down the bowl of the spoon to a stump, and the spoon had to be thrown away. Afterwards, as she cooked, she mourned its departure like that of an old friend. 'A new spoon does not feel the same,' she said.

It was unusual for a farmer's wife to be mean with the food. The recycling of left-overs through the medium of the swill tub or hen run ensured an absence of waste. But it was said that a few of the well-off wives of North Walsham businessmen kept a very tight control over their kitchen store-cupboards. Like Victorian ladies, they carried a collection of keys about their persons and even portioned out the tea and sugar whenever the maids were required to prepare a meal.

In our village, the yardstick of a man's worth was his ability to work. Too much hard work might dull his brain, making him slow of thought and sparing with his words, but idle habits did no good to anyone. If it could be said of an individual that he had not a lazy bone in his body, he was likely to be honest and law-abiding. Light fingers and a lying tongue were regarded as the inevitable by-products of laziness. An honest man or woman would not tell a lie. They either gave you the blunt truth or remained silent if they thought it politic to do so. It did not at all worry them if over-inquisitive 'foreigners' imagined that a blank face was necessarily a sign of rural stupidity, for in early life they had been taught the traditional way to deal with an awkward question: 'Never you know nawthin'. Nobody can't get over that!' their parents had said.

Old people enjoyed telling stories about the strong men they had known, who, as they said, 'put a lot of work behind them'. We heard of a local miller who in the course of his work was able to carry three twenty-stone sacks of flour at a time – one under each arm and a third across his shoulders. Then there was the tale of 'four great men' who, at the end of the day, when rain threatened, decided to work on right through a moonlit night in order to finish harvest. The farmer sent for a barrel of beer, the final stack was laid out and, as the sun came up over the horizon, the last sheaf went into place. While the four were finishing the beer, it began to rain. The men made their way to bed, but the rain continued on and off for six weeks.

The man who came into the yard was recovering from a long illness: 'Look at my hands,' he said, flexing his gnarled fingers. 'All thin and white-looking! They want work.'

Another old couple we knew had lived for most of their married life in a cottage where a strong-growing myrobalan hedge sheltered one side of the garden. When the husband gave up regular farm work, they decided to move nearer to a daughter in the next village, and the cottage remained empty because the landlord thought he could sell the site for building. This state of affairs persisted for some years and the cottage became derelict, but twice a year the old man arrived with his hedging tools to trim the myrobalan. 'I'm seventy year old,' he declared, 'and time's getting short, but I reckon I ha' kept that old mirabella under for fifty year and I aren't a goin' to be beat by it yet.'

In a closely knit community, the few dishonest individuals or families were known and accepted as such. The shops and tradesmen treated them with caution, but their capacity for financial misdoing was limited at a time when hire purchase was virtually unknown and when it was usual to save up one's money until there was enough to pay for whatever it was one wished to buy. 'If you cannot afford it, then Want must be your master!' was what most of the children were told by their parents.

Petty theft was discouraged by the eyes and tongues of neighbours as well as by a wholesome fear of the local policeman. Even at night, our back door was not locked, and a careless farmer could leave an implement in the corner of a field, knowing that it would be in the same place next year, though it might have a little more rust on it and be surrounded by a fresh crop of nettles.

Whenever a farmer had money to spare, he put it back into his farm, using it to buy new machinery or extend his acreage by the purchase of more land. 'Prices may go up or down, but the land is always there,' he would say. 'When times are bad, you can draw in your horns and live off the land.' A countryman liked to stand upon his own ground, and the more he had of it, the better he was satisified. On rare occasions and given the opportunity, this innate urge to acquire land might override a villager's usual standard of honesty.

It is possible that a local carter did not consider it a sin when, over the years, he slowly and laboriously moved the bank of the garden surrounding his isolated cottage until, gaining a few feet each year, he succeeded in bringing into his own enclosure the neglected half-acre of outlying meadow belonging to a farmer in the next parish. Passers-by who realized that a boundary was being moved remained silent. They felt it was none of their business. Fortunately for the carter, the landowner was a tolerant and easy-going man, and when he discovered his loss, he saw the underlying humour of the situation. He contented himself with giving the carter a verbal dressing-down and then offered to settle the matter for payment of a small sum. 'After all, the chap worked hard for that wet old meadow!' was his final comment.

The shops liked to do business on a cash or weekly cash

account basis, but other village tradesmen preferred to send in bills every six months or even once a year as long as they had confidence in their clients. Small tradesmen distrusted the bank and did not fancy keeping too much money in the house, but they liked to feel it was close at hand. It was no good asking the blacksmith for his account: 'That won't hurt you when it come, and I know where the money is when I want it,' was his invariable reply. In the same way, many of the larger transactions in the agricultural world were based upon mutual confidence. The majority of farmers and corn merchants had no written agreements. They bought and sold by word of mouth. When a man said, 'My word is my bond,' he meant it.

At the age of five, village children were sent to Trunch school, and later on they attended one of the larger schools at either Knapton or Mundesley. Education ended at fourteen, and although some of them may not have made much use of it in adult life, they could all read and write and do simple arithmetic. It was an older generation – particularly the girls – who had missed out on book-learning because they were needed at home. Sara Ann was one of those unable to read, though she could just manage to write her name. She was slightly ashamed of this deficiency and, at the same time, regretful. 'They tell me there's some rare good bits in the *News of the World*,' she said.

As soon as I was able to read, father encouraged me to look up unfamiliar words in the dictionary or an encyclopaedia, but otherwise he showed little interest in female education. Two of his sisters were school-mistresses, and maybe early encounters with some of their friends had led him to associate the higher education of women with bossy femininity and the Suffragette movement. For a time mother coped with our lessons, but when I was seven and my brother five, she resorted to a daily governess who taught us for three years until we were sent away to school. As well as practising reading and writing, we learned basic arthimetic, history, geography, drawing and a little French. After one o'clock dinner, the lady disappeared, and for the rest of the day the morning's work was subordinated to an unconscious absorption of the natural world about us. We spent a great deal of time outdoors.

Country children did not realize how lucky they were to be free to roam over such large areas of a relatively safe and friendly environment. We were able to experience Nature rather than make a school study of it, and the textbook followed only after our interest was aroused. If one enjoyed such juvenile wanderings, it was as if the countryside with all its flowers and birds and animals became part of oneself.

We kept a few tame rabbits and a guinea pig, but sometimes our pets were augmented by little animals which the farm men brought to us from the fields. I remember a hedgehog, a limping partridge and a little rabbit – one day, the yard man turned up with his old felt hat full of mallard ducklings. We tended the new arrivals to the best of our ability.

Inevitably, there were deaths, but at least we got to know the creatures around us, and the final burst of childish grief, followed by a consoling funeral under the pear tree, cemented a bond with Nature. One of the aunts was not impressed when she discovered her nephew and niece, prayer-books in hand, conducting the funeral of a baby chicken – a trifle unfair, we thought, when it was she who had first suggested to us a connection between the Almighty and the farmyard. 'Watch the hens round the water trough,' she had said. 'After they have a drink, they raise their beaks to thank God for it.'

Little girls were encouraged to knit, sew and crochet and do simple embroidery and pen-painting. There were plenty of books in the house, and reading became addictive. When you were on your own, a book was like a companion. The landing bookcase contained a number of stories belonging to our parents' youth, and *Children of the New Forest*, *The Swiss Family Robinson* and the works of Louisa M. Alcott rubbed covers with volumes of all the things that *Katy Did* during her Victorian upbringing. Some of those children's books were extraordinarily moral, while others were too sad for words: one gnawed green apples and wept copiously throughout the death-bed scenes in *The Wide, Wide World*, but after the misery was over one felt considerably better, as if purged by the tears. A little later on, I progressed to such authors as Jack London and Ralph Connor and devoured all the splendid African adventure stories of H. Rider Haggard.

Although our early years were surrounded by a happy, busy family life, we were free enough to have individual hobbies and learn to enjoy our own company without becoming introverted. But change had to come. In the autumn of 1920, I was sent to Norwich High School for Girls as a weekly boarder, and from then on life contained other interests and I had friends of my own age. The farm was my home, but the village slipped into a new perspective, and its importance appeared to recede as my world enlarged.